546

EVANGELICAL BELIEFS AND EDUCATIONAL VALUES

This book is dedicated to Helen McEwen and Elizabeth Robinson.

Evangelical Beliefs
and Educational Values

ALEX McEWEN
EARL ROBINSON
School of Education
The Queen's University of Belfast

Avebury

Aldershot • Brookfield USA • Hong Kong • Singapore • Sydney

BR
1640
.M397
1995

Published by
Avebury
Ashgate Publishing Limited
Gower House
Croft Road
Aldershot
Hants GU11 3HR
England

Ashgate Publishing Company
Old Post Road
Brookfield
Vermont 05036
USA

British Library Cataloguing in Publication Data

McEwen, Alex
    Evangelical Beliefs and Educational Values
    I. Title II. Robinson, Earl
    337.1
ISBN 1 85628 671 1

Library of Congress Catalog Card Number: 95-77882

Typeset by
Alastair Edwards
NIESU
The Queen's University of Belfast
Belfast BT7 1NN

Printed and bound by Athenæum Press Ltd.,
Gateshead, Tyne & Wear.

Contents

Abbreviations

AV: Authorised Version

CIM: China Inland Mission

CICCU: Cambridge Inter-Collegiate Christian Union

ESRC: Economic and Social Research Council

IVF: Inter-Varsity Fellowship

IVP: Inter-Varsity Press

JSSR: Journal for the Scientific Study of Religion

KJV: King James Version

MS(S):   Manuscript(s)

NIV: New International Version

NT: New Testament

OMF: Overseas Missionary Fellowship

OT: Old Testament

PESC: The Protestant Ethic and the Spirit of Capitalism

SCM: Student Christian Movement

SU: Scripture Union

UCCF: Universities and Colleges Christian Fellowship

Acknowledgements

The authors are grateful that it was possible to find so many sixth formers and undergraduates who were willing to be interviewed at length or to fill in long questionnaires. In this connection particular thanks are due to our resourceful and indefatigable research assistant Dr Anne Lazenblatt, and to headteachers who generously invited her into their schools, provided her with accommodation and access to pupils. Gratitude is also owed to a number of secretaries of Christian Unions and other religious societies in the higher education sector who co-operated with and facilitated Dr Lazenblatt. Nor must we omit from the scope of our thanks the seven "exemplar" interviewees who were so generous with their time (and in Canada hospitality).

Particular thanks are rendered to John Fairfield of Malaspina College, British Columbia for arranging access, transport and hospitality in various parts of North America, and to Queen's University and the Economic and Social Research Council for assistance with travel and other expenditure.

The ideas expressed here are those of the authors alone and do not necessarily represent the views of Queen's University, the ESRC nor any of those who participated in the project. The research on which this book is based was funded by the ESRC through grant number R000232693.

Myrtle Agus and Scott Harvey were always ready at short notice to wordprocess much material. Alistair Edwards also provided invaluable assistance with tables, diagrams and pagination.

Preface

It does not appear that men will be able to remake the world we have lost, and unless there is a massive change of heart, a veritable revolution in thought and feeling, and a willing surrender of many of the conveniences of modern life and organisation, it is difficult to see how the otherwise irrevocable pattern of social order could be reinfused with religious inspiration. As yet only at the margins and in the interstices, and principally in the domain of private life, has such religious endeavour been effective, in allowing some men, at least, to transcend the present discontents, and in producing, by way of the dissemination of dispositions of goodwill and commitment, that salt of the earth that is necessary to sustain the social order. (B. Wilson, *Religion in Sociological Perspective*, OUP, 1982, p.179.)

Introduction

The research project described in this book grew out of an interest which was stimulated by observing and discussing the Evangelical presence and activities in many Northern Irish schools. Apart from the Roman Catholic sector Northern Irish secondary schools usually have a junior Scripture Union group, recruiting members from the first three forms, and a senior one as well, drawing on forms four, five and six. School notice-boards frequently reveal that these Evangelical groups enjoy a wide range of activities, ranging from formal Bible-study through musical events and quizzes to vacation camps in the United Kingdom or on the continent.

It was noticeable also over the years that teachers' perceptions of Evangelical or Evangelically inclined pupils seemed in general to be favourable, whether with regard to academic progress, industriousness or contribution to extra-curricular activities. There were also interesting accounts of pupils who declined to participate in some of the social activities of schools on the grounds that their beliefs might be compromised.

There seemed to be a fruitful field for research in investigating the nature of the Evangelical way of life and the extent to which it produced what many teachers thought of as "model" pupils. It was of particular interest to see whether structured and sustained Bible-study at lunchtimes, or before or after school, led to any transfer to academic subjects. Of interest also were any tensions or conflicts of an ideological or social nature which were generated at the interface between Evangelicalism and an increasingly secularised ethos in schools and what the resolution of such difficulties might be. It proved possible also to add a comparative dimension to the study by incorporating some insights drawn from research undertaken in North America.

1 Historical and contemporary Evangelicalism

The Protestant ethic

In his book "The Protestant Ethic and the Spirit of Capitalism" (first published in 1904) Max Weber sets out a number of distinguishing features of early Protestant beliefs for their sociological, theological and economic significance. The argument revolves around the impact on social and economic conditions of the Protestant rationalisation of religious ideas, underpinned by their belief in a rational God. Protestant beliefs, in other words, marked a further development in the de-mythologising of God and the rejection of what the early Protestants perceived as priestly magic especially as it was expressed through the sacraments and the priest's power to grant absolution from sins. The traditional Catholic cycle of sin, remorse and absolution was broken by the Protestants' absolute duty to confide in God alone in seeking to attain His grace and ultimately His salvation.

One factor in the emergence of Protestantism was the growing class of independent craftsmen who increasingly attributed their status and power to their individual skills and talents. This led them to question the inherited collectivist authority of priests. They objected to what in effect had become a system of purchasing salvation through the payment of fees for forgiveness and in the rejection of the mystery surrounding priestly services. For the early Protestants, especially the followers of Calvin, the sense of sin became an inner personal burden capable of resolution only through their own personal agency. Puritans, as they were later known, discarded public displays of repentance in preference to individual and private contrition. For Protestants, the logic of accepting God as sole religious confidant was to feel an individual sense of His power, of a direct link between their own consciences and God whom they believed spoke singly to each one of them in guiding their spiritual lives. Such a gift, they felt, liberated them from the horrors of sin and separated them from other men and women who increasingly came to be regarded as "the unregenerate", and who were ultimately and irretrievably destined to damnation. Protestants, by contrast, believed that redemption through faith freed them from a tangible, physical hell without the need for an intercessionist layer of priests. They felt themselves to be no longer under the control of established religious authorities and cleansed of the taint of magic. In summary, their new religion was their destiny; to believe was to be set on the road to a fulfilled life in the community of fellow believers and at the end the prospect of an eternal life.

This new freedom was, however, double-edged in so far as the new religion rejected a doctrine of good works as a means to salvation. Calvin believed that salvation was possible only through faith. Medieval architecture, music and the accumulated wealth and opulence of the Catholic Church were the aesthetic and material outcomes of the traditional belief that salvation could be secured by the endowment by the rich of secular and religious grandeur. Early Protestantism and pre-eminently Calvinism believed that the traditional causal connection between good works and salvation was void since God had already pre-destined some for salvation and others for damnation. In the minds of Calvinists this doctrine corresponded with two groups, the elect and the unregenerate. The doctrine was, however, bleak and uncomforting in so far as certainty about individual destiny could not be obtained during a lifetime and, further, that only a minority of men and women would be chosen for eternal grace. To assume otherwise, Calvinists believed, was a presumption of God's will, that it was open to change through human agency. Calvinism rendered this impossible by posing an unbridgeable gap between God's plan for each person and the ability either to know or alter it. The tolerant and compassionate God of the New Testament, as shown by Jesus's parable of the "Prodigal Son" where he preached that there is rejoicing over the repentance of each sinner, was replaced by a sublime being beyond the compass of human understanding. The Westminster Confession of 1647 sets the doctrine out sombrely as:

> By the degree of God, for the manifestation of His glory, some men and angels are predestined unto everlasting life, and other foreordained to everlasting death. (Chapter III No. 3, first published in 1717).

In this, its strongest form, predestination was quite literally inhuman in its imperviousness to intervention or alteration by believers. Luther's interpretation of a believer's role in determining their fate was a more positive one. He agreed with Calvin that people were inherently sinful and needed God's grace to intervene to move them towards repentance. But Luther stressed the forgiveness and generosity of God's grace whereas Calvin took the doctrine to its logically bleak conclusion framed in such black and white terms.

3

How was such a doctrine to be borne by early believers given the importance and ultimate certainty for good or ill of the after life? The response to this question was that the belief in a predestined fate inevitably became moderated by the imperative of discerning whether or not it was possible to know that membership of the elect had been achieved. This was caused by a form of "salvation panic". It was the prelude to a conceptual shift from a fate immutably ascribed by God to one which was obtainable through upright and purposeful activity in the world. To live such a life, it was believed, removed the greater part of the uncertainty about salvation.

In its fullest form, Calvinism of the sixteenth and seventeenth centuries had become an austere pattern of beliefs which demanded total commitment and great personal discipline of its followers. Salvation had been completely separated from traditional church beliefs and practices especially in their expression through the sacraments. In everyday life this led, for the followers of Calvin, to the elimination of all forms of sensory pleasure as being somehow ungodly and in personal and religious terms an inclination towards a melancholic fatalism.

The calling

The austerity of Calvinism and the individual torment which it engendered concerning salvation and membership of the elect led Protestants to look for assurance that they were chosen through the doctrine of the "calling". Its central feature was the translation of religious beliefs into the daily routine in such a way as to imbue work, family and friendships with God's spirit and to dedicate these and all other aspects of everyday life as a form of worship. Weber describes this as the development of a "worldly asceticism" in complete contrast to medieval monastic life where monks and nuns dedicated their lives to transcending the concerns and affairs of secular life. Weber argues that the creation of such a work ethic among Protestants underpinned paradoxically by a religious ethic renouncing the worldly attractions of wealth, gave an initial and seminal boast to the growth of capitalism as an economic system. For Calvinists, he argues, business and the accumulation of wealth had a profound religious purpose.

Calvinists, however, made a distinction between performing good works to secure salvation and interpreting these as the achievement of signs of God's grace through a "sober and industrious life". The former, they argued, was spiritually arrogant in attempting to know God's will. It was also purposeless since humans were fallible beings and would inevitably fall short of divine standards. Over time, however, the bleakness and uncertainty of a predestined after-life became ameliorated by the acceptance of worldly success in business, craft or profession as evidence of a person's expectation of future salvation.

4

This, it has been argued, gave great "freedom" to the elect (Hill, 1975) since they felt themselves no longer subject, as other men and women were, to the arbitrary forces of society and nature. This related especially to certainty of an eternal life through the elect's comprehension of and oneness with God's purpose. Such spiritual assurance also gave them confidence that their lives' work which they had aligned with God's will, would be blessed by Him and that they would be successful in both this world and the next. Arrogance about salvation was avoided by the belief among Calvinists that there was no absolute certainty that a prosperous calling would lead to its achievement. God was the sole arbiter of those who were chosen. But it was equally strongly believed that the accumulation of wealth and its use in sober and industrious life would not be a barrier to salvation.

The doctrine of the calling in its liberation of men and women from the Catholic Church's doctrinal rules also freed them from its temporal powers. Protestants came to see themselves as a spiritual élite who owed no allegiance to similar social and political elects. Their world was one, Hill argues, where merit as a sign of God's grace replaced traditional hierarchies of birth and religion, whose members were often distinguished by their godlessness. Protestants felt similarly towards the "unregenerate" mass of humanity whom they believed had no calling. By contrast, the converted had the prospect of spiritual and social freedom and by the seventeenth century this was increasingly expressed politically in the challenge to the established authority of the king.

By the early part of that century Puritans had developed strongly held anti-authoritarian views, the outer limits of which were expressed by groups such as the Levellers, Seekers, Ranters and Quakers. Much of this ferment of religious and social upheaval stemmed from both their religious asceticism and their burgeoning economic independence. The link between these two elements of their lives is not self-evident since wealth and spirituality were normally seen as opposites. But for Puritans there was no necessary contradiction because of the nature of their calling since through it they were enjoined to work to glorify God and to interpret any resulting accumulation of wealth as a sign of being chosen as a member of God's elect. Social life was to be similarly fulfilled by endowing daily tasks in the home, at play, or in business with a spiritual purpose. Existential problems concerning the meaning of life and of the world were eliminated since meaning was expressed through labour in God's light.

Christian asceticism and the development of capitalism

Weber summarises Christian asceticism as:

> the rationalisation of conduct within this world, but for the sake of the world beyond, was the consequence of the concept of calling of ascetic Protestantism (Weber, 1985, p. 154).

He also argues that the Protestant Ethic was crucial to the development of capitalism as something more than the pursuit of gain for its own sake. Protestant beliefs gave capitalism what Giddens (1985) calls its "moral energy" by dissociating the pursuit of wealth from its traditional worldly accompaniments or what came to be known in the nineteenth and twentieth centuries as "conspicuous consumption". Wilson summarises the importance of the development of the new religious and cultural asceticism as:

> ..... culturally transformative of western society. Individuals had now an obligation to observe their own conduct carefully, to walk seriously, in the full consciousness that they were God's instruments .... . This powerful demand for new levels of self-control was the basis of the new work order which burgeoned under capitalism. (Wilson, 1982, p.76)

Puritans developed an accounting attitude to life where sin and goodness were set beside each other and the individual's worth expressed according to how these qualities of life balanced. Religious life generally became imbued with commercial metaphors; sin resulted in a "debt" to God with redemption being "bought" through re-dedicating one's life and work to God.

Wealth was thought to be morally suspect only in its potential for misuse through idleness and other worldly forms of pleasure. Puritans were encouraged to pursue and accumulate wealth as a central duty of their calling. In this initial stage of capitalism the Puritan work ethic which emphasised frugality, discipline and the rationality of the labour process, radically altered traditional attitudes towards work and the use of its material rewards. For the great mass of people work was treated as a necessary but important accompaniment of life but one which had little virtue beyond the provision of food and shelter. Great wealth, unless it was sanctioned by or invested in the Church, had traditionally been looked upon as a corrupting influence and especially by Puritans when it was used for what they defined as "irrational" purposes. These were and still are thought of as "idolatry of the flesh". Puritan asceticism overturned contemporary attitudes towards the purpose of work, and the pursuit of wealth and its use through the concept of the calling. Economic success became synonymous with serving God's purpose in the world. It was encouraged and to be sought after in so far as success in business and industry was interpreted as a sign of a more general moral uprightness and religious soundness for membership of the elect.

Weber's argument focuses attention on the fact that capitalism received its initial stimulus from the unintended consequences of a religious ethic which transposed the purely spiritual values of Christian asceticism into business life. It achieved this by making the creation, investment and personal growth of wealth a religious and lifelong duty. This was in contrast, Weber argues, to other world religions which had similar ascetic values such as Hinduism, which focuses on a spirituality beyond this world and in its highest form enjoins followers to transcend material existence through the pursuit of a heightened form of spiritual experience. There is an emphasis on escaping from the concerns of the present life to a preparation for a future re-incarnated existence. The formation and control of the temporal world becomes subsidiary to the attainment of "other worldly" values. In a similar way, Weber argues that in China, which had a long history as a powerful and cultured civilisation, Confucianism through its symbiotic ethic of harmony with the world, acted as a barrier to the development of capitalism. By contrast, the Protestant belief in being "saved" through earthly diligence in anticipation of a heavenly after-life gave it a radical, and, in economic terms, a revolutionary edge.

Its followers in securing salvation had necessarily to change their present material world by achieving the signs of "fitness" for the elect in their personal and business lives. Ideologically, feudal forms of authority embodied especially in the monarchy, were challenged and subsequently overthrown during the English revolution of the seventeenth century by a rising, economically independent class of middle class capitalists. By the seventeenth century Protestant religious liberties had become transposed as individual political rights and economic freedoms and came into conflict with Charles I's recourse to the monarch's divine right to rule as the basis of his authority. Economically, Puritan businessmen objected to the King's monopolistic economic policies on the grounds that they were commercially unfair and restrictive to trade as well as morally corrupt. Politically, Hobbes and Locke argued that a social contract between men based on reason had greater justification than authority based on inherited aristocratic position.

A critique of Weber's theory

The argument surrounding the sources of the Evangelical world view so far has been based on Weber's thesis concerning the primacy of Protestant beliefs in initiating modern capitalism. Formed during the Reformation these had promoted in an incidental way a new and radical economic order underpinned by a religious ethic which sanctioned the accumulation of wealth as a sign of God's grace and ultimately of salvation. In sociological terms, Weber adopts an idealist approach to the initial development of capitalism through his focus on the Protestant rationalising ideal. Early Protestantism rejected what was perceived as the "irrationality" of the Catholic Church, especially its sacerdotal emphasis and the power which the priestly elite had accrued to itself. Weber argued that once the Protestant belief in a rational God took hold it was similarly logical to assume that success in a calling could be taken as a sign of being one of the elect destined for eternal life although prosperity in itself was not seen as the direct means of achieving this. As a result, business and economic life in general, became invigorated with a rationalising ethic which had a directly spiritual purpose as its source and its ultimate end.

The ideational shift in this rationalising process produced a system of labour discipline which gave rise to "the faithful official, clerk, labourer or domestic worker" (Weber, 1985, p.139) It was a system of indoctrination of the lower classes argues Hill:

> Protestant preachers in the late sixteenth and early seventeenth centuries undertook a cultural revolution, an exercise in indoctrination, in brainwashing on a hitherto unprecedented scale. (Hill, 1975, p.324).

Weber makes the point that this new labour process was a result of the combination of economic and religious changes which had occurred during the middle ages and which preceded the advent of Protestantism. There had been, for example, wealthy entrepreneurs in Catholic Italy where the Lombard Bankers supplied venture capital for enterprises throughout Europe and it would be wrong to conclude that Catholicism had been inimical to the development of capitalism. It is reasonable to argue, however, that there was at best ambivalence among the greater number of Catholic clergy towards the accumulation of capital given the sinful opportunities to which traditional consumption led. Far better, it was thought at the time, to endow the Church with the profits arising from the successful use of capital. Amassing personal wealth, for the Puritan, by contrast, had an intrinsic religious value and was interpreted as an indication of God's grace. Giddens (1985) also argues that empirically Weber's thesis is unsupported by evidence concerning the development of capitalism during the sixteenth century in the Netherlands and Switzerland where he argues there was a only a loose relationship between Calvinism and a newer, entrepreneurial form of business life.

Weber, himself, is cautious about over-emphasising the importance of the ascetic Protestantism in transforming medieval culture and introducing rational capitalist forms of economic development. He says that it was "only one side of the causal chain" which led to the development of contemporary western economic systems. Others included factors such as the substantial degree of urbanisation and the rational legal forms of administration largely inherited from the Romans which accompanied it. Neither of these, he suggests, were widespread in eastern societies such as India and China where capitalism had not developed. By the same token, such bureaucratic forms of organisation, he argues, enabled individual nation states to emerge and in time to challenge and gradually to extinguish the feudal authority of the Catholic Church as a pan-European power. It also enabled capitalist enterprises to organise their work methodically in harmony with the administrative ethos of rising nation states. More generally, Protestantism may have been the outward result of an underlying pattern of political and economic change fuelled by the dynamics of the development of nation states during the late middle ages. This raises doubts concerning Weber's central argument that, in addition to the conditions above, ascetic Protestantism was the essential catalyst for the introduction of capitalism. The contrary argument portrays it as an ideological overlay which rationalised underlying economic changes already well established during the middle ages. Marx and Engels offer an alternative view in so far as changes in the class system which inevitably accompany a capitalist form of production require some form of ideological representation through the creation of what they called the "ideal":

> For each new class which puts itself in the place of one ruling before it is compelled to represent the interest as the common interest of all the members of society, that is expressed in ideal form it has to give its ideas the form of universality, and represent them as the only rational, universally valid ones. (Marx and Engels, 1965, p. 62)

Ruling class interests, they argue, are therefore rendered invisible through an ideological transformation which enables the presentation of the dominant culture as the "ideal". Lower classes are thus encouraged or indoctrinated, depending on how well-established the ruling class has become, towards accepting the superiority of the official culture. This is promoted as encompassing the "traditional", "best" or "ideal" patterns of thought and behaviour to which in democracies all may aspire but few will actually achieve. Ascetic Protestantism, following this argument, formed a central ideological element in the consolidation of an emergent and economically dominant class of capitalist entrepreneurs. Its ethic of frugality and self-discipline was held up to the growing subordinate class of wage labourers as a religious duty. This was especially the case in their discouragement of idleness which was perceived as ungodly. It also applied to traditional lower class enjoyment of saints' days, village festivals and sports and freedom of sexual behaviour.

During the 17th century the political ideas of a number of thinkers and radicals, however, provide evidence that within ascetic Protestantism an independent idealist libertarian ethic retained its influence. Winstanley, a leading radical thinker, argued:

No man can be rich but ..... either by his own labours, or by the labour of other men helping him. .... Rich men receive all they have from the labourer's hand, and what they give, they give away other men's labours, not their own. (Hill, 1975, p. 33.)

Ascetic Protestantism as an endowment of spirituality to capitalism had, nevertheless, a limited life once the forces of production took hold. Weber acknowledges this:

when asceticism was carried out of monastic cells into everyday life, and began to dominate worldly morality it did its part in building the tremendous cosmos of the modern economic order .... victorious capitalism, since it rests on mechanical foundations, needs its support no longer ..... the idea of duty in one's calling prowls about in our lives like the ghost of dead religious beliefs. (Weber, 1985, pp.181-182.)

Part of the "mechanical foundation" came from the Puritans' openness to new developments in science as an aspect of man's duty, according to God's will, to work actively to transform the world. Wilson (1982) suggests that "mastery" was a central feature of Puritans' acceptance of science which then enabled them to fulfil their spiritual purpose by both transforming the physical world and pursuing their social and commercial enterprises. The adoption of science, initially as an aspect of the calling, was to have far-reaching consequences. It gave the process of secularisation a powerful boost through its essentially reductionist purpose of eliminating metaphysical explanations of the cosmos. The core rationalising dynamic of Puritans' religious beliefs, which was conducive to science, paradoxically laid the foundation for undermining those beliefs as a scientific worldview came to dominate the post medieval world. It also raised problems for Puritans and Christianity in general as witches, evil spirits, Hell and the devil became de-mythologised as the causes of suffering and sin. These traditional sources of blame, if eliminated, meant that individuals had to look inwards to themselves as the source of evil and wrongdoing. The gap between belief and science was increasingly filled by the Puritan's sense of guilt.

Wesley and modern Evangelicalism

Modern Evangelicals today look back to the stalwarts of the Reformation period with a sense of affinity and regard themselves as their spiritual descendants. The theological debates and controversies, however, which engaged Luther, Melanchthon, Bucer, Oecolampadius and Calvin no longer constitute burning issues; predestination has been shelved, and is not permitted to be a divisive question. The problem of the real presence of the body and blood of Christ in communion is a matter about which Evangelicals can agree to differ; yet this was such a burning issue at the time of the Reformation that at the Marburg colloquy Luther felt unable to give Zwingli the "right hand of fellowship" (Galatians 2:9 NIV) on the matter. (Atkinson, 1968, p.98.)

Evangelicalism may in a very definite sense rest on a set of fundamental principles established during the Reformation but its distinctive twentieth century shape owes much to other contributory influences, such as the impact of the Enlightenment, the subsequent higher biblical criticism and its responses to them. The ideological structure of Evangelicalism therefore needs to be viewed in the context of the backcloth of the mostly secularising forces against which Evangelicals have felt the need to defend their views. The importance of belief in the inerrancy of scripture, for example, is related to the Evangelical comment on the higher biblical criticism, particularly as practised in Germany. To Evangelicals it seemed utterly perverse, in the face of a world needing to hear the good news, to speculate about the possible multiple authorship of the Pentateuch (the first five books of the Old Testament), as did the scholar Julius Wallhausen. Nor have the twentieth century descendants of Wallhausen, Dibelius, Bultmann, Käsemann and Bornkamm been any more acceptable to Evangelicals, who feel that the attempt to demythologise the Christian faith and to re-express it in existential categories is deplorable.

If, however, there is a central, dominant concept in modern Evangelicalism then perhaps it is to be found in the notion of assurance. This idea would have been expressed in mediaeval Latin as "certitudo salutis", and today would be exemplified in hymns such as,

> Blessed assurance, Jesus is Mine,
> O What a foretaste of glory divine,
> (Frances Jane van Alstyne 1820 - 1915 in Christian Hymns. Evangelical Movement of Wales, 1977)

or

> I know not why God's wondrous grace
> To me has been made known
> Nor why, unworthy, as I am,
> He claimed me for His own
> But I know whom I have believed
> And am persuaded, that He is able
> To keep that which I've committed
> Unto Him against that day.
> (Daniel Webster White 1840 - 1891 in Christian Hymns Evangelical Movement of Wales)

There has always existed a concept of assurance amongst Christians and it can be clearly seen in the way in which early Christians, such as Felicity and Perpetua, died with serenity in the arena at Carthage or Blandina being burned alive at Lugdunum, who was nevertheless able to forgive her tormentors. But in modern times, it is in the work of John Wesley that the note of triumphant assurance is heard most clearly, and he has left an indelible impression on subsequent Evangelicalism.

Pristine Calvinism, as has been pointed out, taught that no-one could be really sure whether he or she was of the elect. One could only entertain a Godly hope and scrutinise one's life to find those signs which made a "calling and election sure". (2 Peter 1:10 AV) In the whole area of predestination, of determinism, the religious thinkers of the sixteenth and seventeenth centuries placed different sorts of interpretations on the scriptural data. Depending on the type of meaning that became accepted differing scriptural emphases emerged. For Calvin a passage such as Romans 9:16, 21 NIV was central to his theological viewpoint.

> It does not, therefore depend on man's desire or effort, but on God's mercy
> .... God has mercy on whom He wants to have mercy, and He hardens
> whom He wants to harden.

Later Calvinist doctrinal formulations picked up the sense of the above passage from Romans and transposed it in, for example, Chapter III of the Westminster Confession of 1647 as quoted earlier.

Other thinkers placed on scripture an interpretive and liberating frame which gave prominence to the notion of foreknowledge, as contained in Romans 8:29 NIV:

> For those God foreknew He also predestined to be conformed to the likeness
> of His Son,

and to the idea of "whosoever will" as contained in John 3:16 NIV:

> For God so loved the world that He gave His only Son, that whosoever
> believes in Him shall not perish but have eternal life.

There is an inevitable tension between the notion of an immutable decree, made by God either before or after the Fall of Adam, as to the identity of the elect, and the idea of a gospel freely offering pardon to all with the real possibility that all might accept. Other consequences also flowed from the dichotomy. Calvinism came to believe and teach a limited theology of atonement; that Christ died for the elect (and only the elect). Wesley and most of his followers, who believed in "whosoever will, may come" as a slogan, went much further in the teaching that Christ died for all and that God, being supra-temporal simply knew in advance those who would choose His gracious offer of forgiveness and "the gift of eternal life". Weber, commenting on the tension between the two viewpoints, remarks tersely:

> It is unnecessary for us here to analyse the various inconsistent attempts to combine with the predestination and providence of God the responsibility and free will of the individual. They began as early as in Augustine's first attempt to develop the doctrine. (Weber, 1985, p.221.)

In the course of preliminary discussion about the present research, a teacher, who had formerly held Evangelical beliefs provided some insights into the way in which an idea of assurance still affects pupils. She had been approached by a group of fourth form girls, members of the school Scripture Union group and from predominantly Evangelical backgrounds. They were very fond of their English teacher, who was a devout Roman Catholic, and after a discussion in an English class about matters eternal they had discovered, to their amazement, and horror, that she was unable to say definitely that she was going to heaven. She had tried to explain to them the Roman Catholic teaching about presumption; that Christians should be humble, like the tax collector, in the parable of the Pharisee and the tax collector who would not even look up to heaven, but beat his breast and said "God have mercy on me, a sinner" and that we should not presumptuously and arrogantly claim to be going to heaven. But the pupils were clear about their spiritual position: they knew that their sins were forgiven, that they were going to heaven, that the Lord was in their hearts and that they were happy to testify to this. Wesley's religion was very much like this, a matter of the heart, and Methodism has since been characterised by a reluctance to argue about theological niceties. As a movement it has been more committed to worship and evangelism than to systematic theology.

Another abiding influence which Wesley left to modern Evangelicalism was a concern about sanctification. Some of his more enthusiastic followers in fact articulated a doctrine of sinless perfectionism, which meant that believers progressed in Christian living to the point where they were without sin. The various "Holiness Churches" which sprang up in the late nineteenth and early twentieth centuries would have drawn inspiration from such a view. Sanctification represented the process by which the indwelling Holy Spirit gradually cleansed a believer's life, and was the inward and experiential correlate of the outward doctrine of justification whereby God graciously declared a sinner to be in the right with Him. In harmony with the Wesleyan teaching on sanctification modern Evangelicals would regard addiction to tobacco or alcohol or being sexually promiscuous as signs of an unsanctified life.

Sociologically, it can be argued that Wesley was doing for working people what Calvin had accomplished for the bourgeoisie, albeit without the engine of God's "double decree", (although his fellow evangelist Whitefield was a

Calvinist). He taught his converts how to organise and administer, to plan and manage their time, to control alcohol, to cherish their families, and to conduct regular Bible study sessions. He was proud of how his message revolutionised the lives of men who had been drunken wife-beaters and spoke of "lions who had turned into lambs".

Two innovations in particular call for attention: the institution of the class and the notion of the circuit. The class, numbering about a dozen and with a leader who collected the pennies each week, met regularly for Bible Study. They also monitored each other's sanctification so that perceived misbehaviours were disapproved of and eliminated. The circuit was really a means of administering separated groups in localities and of exposing members to mobile evangelistic and ministering talent. One of the reasons for Methodism's success in the United States was the manner in which the circuit riders ministered to 'folk' on the frontier. Although Wesley never left the Established Church and Methodism as a movement only made the inevitable break four years after his death, his rationalising innovations were of a secularising kind.

This view is based on the Berger paradigm (1969) that a monopolistic sacred canopy is a strong one and that pluralism brings with it secularisation.   To Berger the "sacred canopy" consists of the meanings which people project on to the cosmos. These meanings take on, for humankind, an objective existence "out there" and are, in his words, "objectivated". To objectivate meanings in this way, as opposed to the chaotic void of the universe, sustains humankind in the struggle against anomie or spiritual breakdown.   Berger argues that the mediaeval church exercised a monopoly over the projected meanings and controlled them strictly. If, for example, like Huss in Bohemia or Galileo in Italy, you challenged the accepted world-view with a set of countervailing meanings you were likely to end up being burned at the stake or threatened with torture. But the Renaissance and the Reformation shattered the monopoly; other "sacred canopies" emerged commanding the total allegiance of their followers and in Berger's view such a dilution of a monopolistic and unitary "sacred canopy" opens up channels through which secularising innovations flow. To cite but one example, it is an anthropological commonplace that shamanistic or priestly élites tend to distance themselves from the common herd and employ distancing strategies to do so. In the thirteenth century the church codified the ideal of virginity of I Corinthians Chapter 7 into a ruling that priests were henceforth to be celibate; when Martin Luther broke with Rome one of the first things he did was to marry a nun. This was an example followed by thousands of those who abandoned the Roman priesthood. It is also a secularising and de-mystifying action. The Bergerian paradigm has however been challenged by R. Stark and J. C. McCann who argue that:

The traditional paradigm in the sociology of religion sees strength in religious monopolies, attributing to them the ability to sustain an unchallenged, taken for granted, sacred canopy. The newer paradigm regards religious monopolies as weak, locating religion's vitality in pluralism and competition. A crucial test of these competing paradigms arises in the hypothesis that rank and file Catholic commitment varies inversely to the proportion of nominally Catholic within any appropriate set of units of analysis. Results based on the 102 Roman Catholic dioceses of the United States show that ordination rates, the ratio of priests to nominal Catholics, and Catholic school enrolment are proportionately highest where Catholics are few. Results based on the 50 states show the same inverse relationship between the per cent Catholic and the ratio of priests to Catholics (Stark and McCann, 1993, p.111.)

In their concluding discussion they argue:

> these findings add substantially to the burden of contrary evidence that is bringing down the theoretical paradigm that so long dominated the sociology of religion (p.121).

It may be that the tension between the two ideological paradigms reflects the differing geographical and socio-historical backcloths against which they are set, one European and the other American, and eclectic use needs to be made of them as explanatory tools.

As far back as Niebuhr's work on the second generation transition from sect to denomination, studies of religiosity in North America have shown that differences between European and North American practice reflect differing geographical, political, socio-economic and demographic backgrounds. Secularisation theory, for example, has to take account of the fact that substantially higher rates of church attendance in Northern America are related to the position of churches in North America as foci for what in Europe would be regarded a secular activities. This may be particularly so where churches continue to function as signifiers of ethnicity, such as for example, those of Ukrainian Orthodox believers.

According to Berger's paradigm, Wesley was shifting the focus of interest away from patterns of religious behaviour in which a priestly élite played a dominant role towards religious activities dominated by laity. In terms of everyday life, pietistic and moral behaviour under Wesley began to bulk more importantly than the various kinds of liturgical or sacramental acts which depend on priests. The essence of a sacramental act lies in its mystery; the host is elevated followed by the sacred words and the miracle of trans-substantiation takes place. Critics of Christian sacramentalism argue that there is a continuum represented by such activities which at its other end shades over into sacrificial

15

blood running down altars, or initiates consuming the flesh of the totem ancestor. Any move away from such age-old concepts can therefore be construed as a secularising one. The gradual slippage from a miraculous mass or communion feast to one purely of remembrance is neatly paralleled in the Methodist preference for non-fermented wine in the chalice (the argument put forward for this pertained to converted alcoholics). Wesley was also aware of the spiritual dangers inherent in a situation wherein by his encouragement of frugality, thrift and self-control he was leading people to amass wealth.

Evangelicals have as a whole body generally tended not to overemphasise the sacramental and the sacerdotal. And although they are to be found in large numbers in the mainline churches this is not usually out of strong conviction as to a particular church polity. The Anglican church as a whole, for instance, supports episcopacy, the fact of there being bishops, as well as presbyters and deacons. Anglican Evangelicals would argue, however, that episcopacy is of the "bene esse" or well being of the church, whereas Anglo-Catholics would argue for the "esse" or essentiality of bishops. Anglican Evangelicals, in other words, view episcopacy pragmatically, as a useful way of administering a church, whereas Anglo-Catholics would see it as essential to the nature and tone of the church and representing the mind of God to its followers. For many Evangelical Anglicans the Church of England as well as the world-wide Anglican communion constitute a large pool in which to "fish" for souls. The Evangelical world has its own network of interlocking societies, printing houses, Bible colleges and conferences which function as a kind of "church within a church". Some groups of Evangelicals are of course to be found organised as "gathered churches" and with an articulated doctrine of separation from the world. In general, the members of a University Christian Union or a school Scripture Union group or a neighbourhood Crusaders would have as organisers and participants more members from Anglican, United Reformed or Methodist circles than from, say, the Elim Pentecostal or the Christian Brethren. The "church within a church" effect would be reinforced in that the officers of such groups would be expected to sign a detailed doctrinal credo as a guarantee of ideological purity and soundness. This is similar to the position where a practising member of a mainline church, who regularly recites the Apostles' or Nicene creeds, might if he or she wished to join an Evangelical missionary society be required to subscribe to the:

> inerrancy of Holy Scripture, not only in matters pertaining to faith and morals, but also in those pertaining to history, geography and science.

Perhaps the feature of modern Evangelicalism which most resonates back to Wesley is that of the itinerant evangelist such as Billy Graham or Oral Roberts. Prolonged altar calls of the Billy Graham-type, urging potential converts to "make their decision for Christ" always point in a Wesleyan or Arminian direction, rather than a Calvinist one. Where a Calvinist theology is strongly in the background it would be felt that altar calls are unnecessary in that the Holy Spirit will be at work anyway, calling out the elect.

The Evangelical following attracted by popular Evangelicals such as Billy Graham and the success of their preaching in recruiting converts may be related to the sociological commonplace that priestly élites tend to render matters concerning the sacred arcane. It is in the nature of a sacerdotal caste that to preserve its authority it must surround itself with an air of mystery and distance itself from the common man. But when there is a mass demand for assurance and salvation then it has often been the Evangelical revivalist who has stepped into the gap with a plain and straightforward message. The great evangelists have gone where the people are and made it easy for the masses of the people to hear their message. In this they could be said to be emulating the first great travelling evangelist, Paul of Tarsus. In taking over Harringay Arena or Wembley Stadium or the California Superbowl to preach the gospel to the multitudes Billy Graham is directly in the succession of Whitefield and Wesley, who, when denied access to Anglican Cathedrals, took to the fields to address the masses. Historians and sociologists often try to relate well-known religious revivals to underlying socio-economic stresses in particular societies and hypotheses may be more or less convincingly argued along these lines.

It is possible, for example, to argue that the great American camp revivals of the nineteenth century, where the preaching of itinerant evangelists such as Finney was accompanied by phenomena such as mass swooning, called by the preachers "being slain of the Lord", is directly related to the loneliness and stress of frontier life, of civilising a wilderness. It could be argued, by contrast, that salvation imperatives are a perennial feature of human existence and that every so often, even in the midst of secularising processes, the need to be protected from anomie and to have a religious set of meanings explaining the universe, the meaning of life and the afterlife will produce the kind of mass demand which revivalist preaching satisfies.

With the advent of "tele-evangelism" in the United States one can see how revivalist techniques can produce mass movements and can become institutionalised and powerful enough to form potent political lobbies. Such lobbies and the evangelists who spearhead them also present a curious paradox from the perspective of secularisation theory. Whilst the evangelists and their followers might be thought to be theologically retarded, the techniques of mass evangelism, as exemplified by the Billy Graham crusades, are thoroughly up-to-date, and organisationally in the marketing spirit of multi-nationals. Recent empirical research would support the notion of relative retardation in attitudinal terms. Schmalzbauer (1993) discusses the "new class" or "knowledge class". This new class has been broadly conceptualized so as to include all professionals

17

and managers and more narrowly to include only those who work in cultural production such as academia and journalism. Schmalzbauer opts for the broader definition and his argument, supported by his research findings, is that Evangelical "new class" workers resist the liberalising effect of upward social mobility. Non-Evangelical "new class" workers in general tend to adopt more liberal value positions along a range of issues such as abortion, homosexuality, sexual mores, American foreign policy and to move away from traditional, entrenched class positions on such issues. As members of this class, Evangelicals might be expected to show similar movement but in fact exhibit considerable resistance to the values shift.

The religious subculture which exerts such a potent effect of retardation, with respect to sexual mores, for example, is also the culture which in "tele-evangelism" and international crusades employs the most sophisticated public relations and marketing techniques. There is a paradox here which resonates as far back as Tyndale who was forced in the sixteenth century to flee to Holland to complete and publish his translation of the Bible. In the face of sustained opposition from the law, copies of his bible in the vernacular were smuggled into England through the Port of London in bales of merchandise, by big business, in fact, the then equivalent of multi-nationals.

Wesley bestrides a mid-way position between Tyndale and Billy Graham in so far as he and his associates generated a tradition of triumphant and joyful evangelism which runs through the great Victorian and Edwardian revivalists and culminates in the great popular evangelists of the late twentieth century. It is also significant that in the two way traffic across the Atlantic the majority part of the movement has been from America, the home of capitalism in the nineteenth and twentieth centuries to Europe. Moody, Sankey and Finney all toured the British Isles in the late nineteenth century and attracted much publicity. "Moody and Sankey" as a phrase still connotes musical revivalism. Moody was a gifted Chigago orator and Sankey a talented singer, and Sankey's hymns would be still regarded as the tunes of "that old time religion". British home grown evangelists did travel but perhaps did not have the international impact nor emotional appeal of their transatlantic counterparts.

In discussing the phenomenon of the modern evangelist, Roy Coad, (1968) a historian of the Christian Brethren, laments the fact that when Evangelical churches have combined to organise a local crusade they often feel hurt when their liberal fellow churchmen cold-shoulder the invited evangelist and refuse to support the crusade, "as if a cloud had passed across the sun". (p.285.)

It is arguable that the most potent factor in shaping modern Evangelicalism, particularly in terms of its ideology, is its negative reaction to intellectual changes of the nineteenth and early twentieth centuries. Berger (1969), in a discussion of the "ebb and flow" of secularisation, selects 1799 as an important date. This was the year when the German thinker Schleiermacher made his "Address to the Cultured Despisers", that is, his message to those intellectuals who as a result of the Enlightenment no longer believed in but despised Christianity. Through it he initiated a kind of secularising, bargaining process; in effect, to pare down the miraculous element in Christianity, such as the Virgin Birth, but to retain the ethical teaching of Jesus. Berger is concerned to argue that secularising change does not take place in a vacuum; the Schleiermachian type of "compromising" theology fitted well into the great era of "Kulturprotestantismus", the time when the affluent European bourgeoisie was becoming steadily richer and was enjoying its music and philosophy and literature. But the traumas of the Great War, the Depression and the rise of Naziism dealt such a devastating blow to the underlying socio-economic plausibility structure that a more transcendent theology gained prominence. This was the work of Karl Barth, with his emphasis on the "otherness" of God, His gracious descent to man, and man's inability to reach up to God via reason or natural theology. It has been famously said (J. McConnachie, 1931) that Barth's "Römerbrief", his commentary on the book of Romans, published in 1918;"fell like a bomb on the playground of the theologians". (p.43.) There had been during the nineteenth century an attempt to apply reason to scripture, to write "lives of Jesus" which attempted to rationalise the New Testament accounts by sieving out the legendary material, but which somehow ended up by making Jesus into a Victorian gentleman. Barth's was an approach to theology which spoke of God's gracious descent to man, and of His word as heard in scripture. He himself recounted how he felt at the time like someone climbing inside a bell-tower and clutching at an end of rope and suddenly finding himself tolling a mighty bell. (see Hoyle, 1930, pp.72-73.)

In the wake of Barth there grew up in Europe and America the Biblical Theology movement. This was in the tradition of Schleiermacher, in accepting the latest findings of higher criticism of the bible, but it also followed Barth in that it endeavoured to ascertain what the Divine word actually meant to an Amos in his whole historical and socio-cultural setting and then to extrapolate from such words a universal meaning for all people for all time. In terms of secularisation therefore, there was more of ebb perhaps than of flow involved in it. Barth and his friends as they watched the course of events in Germany in the early thirties, the chancellorship of Hitler, the Reichstag fire and the spread of Nazism, felt compelled to speak their minds, which they did at Barmen in 1934, in the words of the Synod of Barmen declaration. The declaration openly opposed Fascism and as a result Barth and his friends of what was known as the "Confessing Church" had to move to Switzerland, Barth being deprived of a Chair in Bonn in 1935.

After the Second World War, however, came the German economic miracle of the fifties and sixties. This coincided with the rise in popularity of Bultmann's theology which is a secularising one in that the former objective verities or religio-factual truths are reinterpreted in existential categories. The Resurrection, for example, is no longer viewed as in any sense a real physical event, describable in historical terms, but is correlated with a change in individual consciousness wherein "authentic living" is realised. Human persons, in other words, hearing the gospel story preached, come to the realisation that they are not alone in a meaningless void, but that the cosmos is a gracious gift from God into which people can put their trust and can thereafter live without anxiety or fear.

In the late sixties there appeared the "Death of God" theologians. The Bishop of Woolwich, the late J.A.T. Robinson, had written a popular paperback in 1963 entitled "Honest to God" in which he tried to replace what he termed the "supranaturalist projection" with depth imagery. Such imagery chimed in well with the kind of view espoused by the American theologian Paul Tillich who spoke of God as "the ground of our Being". Later writers such as Van Buren and Harvey Cox were to question the usefulness of "God" language at all. If *Weltanschauungen*, or pictures of reality, or world-views, are important to people, and the spread of fundamentalisms suggests that some pictures of reality are indeed almost impossible to dislodge, then in Berger's words the functions of bishops, or shamans, or high-priests is to act as reality policemen. This occurs when an earthquake destroys half a city and many die, and people are threatened with anomie in the face of the impossibility of explaining the purpose of such loss of life. Then the reality police arrive and speak of the inscrutable will of God. Faith is restored and the cosmos is given "nomos" or meaningful structure, once again. There is then something faintly anomalous in a situation so secularising that senior reality policemen deny the existence of God or repudiate the notions of any transcendent world with which our cosmos may be related.

In the face of all these varying changes of emphasis, whether theological, sociological or philosophical, Evangelicals have a firm tradition running right back to the Lollards and beyond, a tradition in which scripture is of the utmost importance, being "God's Word Written". Broadbent (1931) in "The Pilgrim Church" attempts to show that down through the centuries there has always been an unofficial strand of Christianity represented by Churches such as those of the Waldenses or Vaudois in the mountains of Switzerland, or Bohemia or Italy, in which the scriptures were accessible to believers. But in the world at large, at the time of the Reformation, they had to be wrested away from priestly élites and delivered to the people of Europe in their vernaculars. Since the rise of the Protestant missionary movements there has also been the continuing effort to put the scriptures into the hands of the people of the world in their own languages. Evangelicals were and are still concerned with matters eternal, with the salvation of souls, in the spirit of 2 Timothy 3:14 NIV:

> But, as for you, continue in what you have learned and become convinced of, because you know those from whom you learned it and how from infancy you have known the holy scriptures which are able to make you wise for salvation through faith in Jesus Christ.

Christopher Hill, 1993, from a non-Christian viewpoint, in "The English Bible and the Seventeenth Century Revolution" illustrates what a potent document the Bible can be when placed in the hands of the common people. The emphasis on the authority of scripture is also reinforced by the conviction that it speaks "una voce". One of Billy Graham's favourite phrases is "The Bible teaches that". A senior figure on the English Evangelical scene, John Stott has this to say:

> I think I would characterise Evangelicals as those who, because they identify Scripture as God's word, are deeply concerned to submit to its authority in their lives (whatever their precise formulation of the doctrine may be). (John Stott, 1988, p.104.)

In other words, the hallmark of Evangelicals is not so much an impeccable set of words as a submissive spirit, namely their a priori resolve to believe and obey whatever scripture may be shown to teach.

Over against such an attitude to scripture and to its authority as thus conceived Professor J. Barr in a book published in 1977 extracted from a defined corpus of Evangelical theological writing a set of beliefs centred, he alleged, on the concept of biblical inerrancy. This, he argued, is the lynchpin of Evangelical beliefs and he entitled the book "Fundamentalism". The epithet "fundamentalist" is derived from the collective title of a set of twelve books called "The Fundamentals", published in the USA from 1910 on, containing articles, as F. F. Bruce says:

> in defence of the Christian faith by a variety of eminent Evangelical scholars.

F.F. Bruce goes on to argue that:

> Nowadays the term is commonly used to denote one who holds extreme traditionalist and literal views and has been well called 'a refined theological swear word'. (F.F. Bruce, 1964, p.206.)

Clearly, from within the Evangelical fold the adjective "fundamentalist" when used to describe their beliefs, is held to have a pejorative overtone and is rejected by them. Edwards and Stott (1988) refer to an exchange of correspondence with J. Barr in which Stott rejects the appellation "fundamentalist", with Barr grudgingly conceding, but adding the rider that there is a very great overlap between fundamentalism, as he perceives it, and Stott's Evangelicalism. (p.89.) Plainly Evangelical beliefs and definitions of Evangelicalism lie along a spectrum, just as Evangelical behaviours range from the quietistic pietism of the Hutterites to the social activism of the Salvation Army.

The late F.F. Bruce, who occupied the prestigious Ryland's Chair of Biblical Criticism at Manchester University for many years, was a member of the Christian Brethren. He was the successor to the Baptist scholar, H.H. Rowley, and the Presbyterian T.W. Manson, and a prolific author, with a major contribution to the corpus characterised as fundamentalist theology although his eirenic and conciliatory scholarship was above any particular sectional spirit. He explicitly disavowed the definition "conservative Evangelical", preferring, as he put it, to remain "unhyphenated". (1964, p. 204.)

Edwards and Stott in their dialogue also reveal the extent to which the Evangelical apologetic has come to terms with radical theology, and it could be argued that the point at which contemporary Evangelical ideology begins was in 1953 with the first edition of the Inter-Varsity Fellowship Bible Commentary (published by IVF). At about the same time, John Laing, (later Sir John) built Tyndale House at Cambridge to facilitate Evangelical scholars, particularly with regard to the publication of the series of Tyndale commentaries on each book of the Bible, the first to appear being Leon Morris's "Thessalonians" in 1956. The ideological shift represented by the new-look Evangelical apologetic was more substantively a matter of tone and style than of dilution of the old certainties, nor was the change confined to Europe. In North America the term neo-Evangelicalism came into use. Referring to this usage F.F. Bruce remarks:

> It is a term which has significance only in an American context. It has been devised to indicate not a deviation from evangelicalism as commonly understood, but certain features of method, approach, co-operation and so forth which have not traditionally characterised evangelicalism in the United States. (F.F. Bruce, 1964, p.203.)

If the ideology of Evangelicalism is represented by its scholars, writing for both religious and secular presses, its social networks function through societies such as the Universities and Colleges Christian Fellowship, the Scripture Union, the Crusaders movement, through Bible Colleges such as London Bible College, or Fuller in Pasadena, California or Regent College in Vancouver. It is also expressed through missionary societies of both general type such as the Overseas Missionary Fellowship and of a more functional nature such as the Missionary Aviation Fellowship, who act as a service group to others or the translator group, the Wycliffe Bible Translators.

A further integral feature of Evangelical practice, particularly as it applies to some of its missionary societies is the concept of "living by faith" with regard to financial resources. The Overseas Missionary Fellowship,[1] for example, still follows the ethos of its founder, Hudson Taylor, in that it does not publicise its financial needs or its plans. If it is thought desirable to build a hospital, for example, then it is left to God to supply the need invisibly and no building programme is commenced until the funding is in the bank.

Evangelical apologists would argue that instances of this kind of "living by faith" are proof of the miraculous intervention of God in the furtherance of the Evangelical cause but from a sociological point of view it is possible to argue that the population of Evangelicals world-wide forms a definite and observable constituency and that members by and large believe in practices such as tithing, giving a tenth of their disposable income "to the Lord's work", and that given that there is a finite number of missionary societies, the distribution of gifts is going to match the needs. When particular, perceived needs are met, anonymously or otherwise, the Evangelical response may be to say "God has provided" and on the other hand when money does not turn up to say "God is testing our faith".

Evangelical lore abounds with accounts of businessmen who decided to increase their giving from a tithe to a third and saw God prosper their efforts even more, to the extent that apparently, the more they gave the more successful their businesses became. But a more pedestrian explanation of such happenings may be that from the very beginning they were extremely efficient and successful entrepreneurial capitalists and that the combination of a strict Evangelical way of life with shrewd business acumen meant that profits increased so that they were able to give more and more of their income to Evangelical causes. In addition, the skilled manual worker's tithing will be in relation to money saved through his abstinence from say, tobacco, alcohol or the football pools, in which his peers take enjoyment. Evangelicalism in the case of the manual worker, has often been perceived as the first rung of the upward social mobility ladder, so that the next generation of children will experience increasing prosperity. Some of the sixth form interviewees to whom we spoke were the children of blue collar Pentecostals, and, scrutinising parental occupations and general family background, it was clear that the social mobility factor was present when comparing pupils' levels of education and career aspirations with those of their parents.

No description of the contemporary Evangelical world would be complete without mentioning the Charismatic movement. This takes its name from its interest in the charismatic or spiritual gifts mentioned in 1 Corinthians 12:4 NIV:

> There are different kinds of gifts, but the one Spirit.

This movement was initially associated with Episcopalian and Roman Catholic circles in the United States and from there spread during the sixties, in such circles, to Europe. It is an Evangelical movement in that it is very much "of the heart", in Wesleyan terms, but has different emphases from the main bodies of Evangelicalism. It welcomes Roman Catholic members without requiring any credal adjustment and it does not frown at moderate consumption of wine. It shares a similar attitude to Christian initiation as that of classical Pentecostalism; salvation is through repentance from sin and faith towards God, and is followed by baptism in water by immersion and the second experience of the "Baptism in the Holy Spirit", often accompanied by "speaking in tongues", or glossolalia. This position would not be inflexibly adhered to; recent publications, such as "Pentecostal Anglicans" would indicate that Anglican or Roman Catholic infant baptism is acceptable. The second experience is also regarded as a reviving one, resembling the more standard form of Evangelical conversion but glossolalia is no longer regarded as a necessary sign of renewal. The movement has grown substantially and the sociologist Danièle Hervieu - Léger has estimated a membership of 200,000 in France either on a regular or occasional basis of meeting in 1987. (Gilles Kepel, 1994, p.76.)

A significant number of Charismatics have seceded from mainline churches to form "house-churches" on the grounds that Christians have no duty to be "Keepers of museums", and in pursuance of what is perceived to be in the spirit of the New Testament. The text Romans 16:3-5 NIV would be regarded as seminal:

> Greet Priscilla and Aquila, my fellow-workers in Christ Jesus. They risked their lives for me. Not only I but all the churches of the Gentiles are grateful to them. Greet also the church that meets at their house.

For a while parts of the Charismatic movement were characterised by the phenomenon known as "shepherding" or "discipling" which involved recruits being assigned to mentors. Much controversy was occasioned by this practice and it seems to have been abandoned. Embarrassment was caused to the house-church movement in Ulster because the doctrine committee of the Presbyterian church published a paper critical of the practice. Stories had begun to circulate about medical students abandoning their studies in order to undertake gardening duties for leaders of particular house-churches, and, as Presbyterian congregations had been particularly affected, the church as a whole felt compelled to speak.

In general terms, secularisation theory has to accommodate the fact that surveys of religious belief indicate that a substantial majority of people retain a belief in God and in practices such as prayer, even if they are non-church going. In particular terms, where a moribund church is taken over by Charismatics it seems to increase rapidly in numbers. The network of house-churches and Christian schools that is fast developing in the Western world would indicate that currently the charismatic type of Christianity is both increasing in its own terms and in having an enlivening effect on more traditional Christian bodies. The present archbishop of Canterbury is dismissed by some of the tabloid papers as a "happy clapper", but it was the hard-headed Mrs Thatcher who supported him for the See of Canterbury because he could fill churches with people and to a Prime Minister who saw the market as applying to all areas of life such a reputation was high praise indeed.

In postulating that twenty first century Evangelicalism stands in a succession that ultimately runs back to Wesley and Calvin and that both of these have made a substantial impact on the development of the movement, one encounters the difficulty of the ideological tension existing between the two leaders. Wesley's concept of universal grace seems a far remove from Calvin's immutable divine decree of predestination. Weber was aware of this difficulty but discounts it:

> the aspiration to the higher life, the second blessedness, served it as a sort of makeshift for the doctrine of predestination. Moreover, being English in origin its ethical practice was closely related to English Puritanism, the revival of which it aspired to be. (Weber, 1985, p.142.)

Weber appears to be arguing here that the demands of Wesley's doctrine of sanctification generated for believers the same kind of tension as had the scrutinising of one's life for Calvinists. He adds:

> The signs given by conduct which formed an indispensable means of ascertaining true conversion, even its condition, as Wesley occasionally says, were in fact just the same as those of Calvinism. (p.143.)

Also, another side of the coin from universal grace and assurance of present salvation was the Wesleyan teaching that one could "fall from grace" (Galatians 5:4 AV) and lose salvation. this was an enormous spur to moral effort and, Weber points out, acted similarly, as a sort of moral/spiritual engine to drive a diligent and frugal way of life.

In the nineteenth and twentieth centuries , it has been argued, Evangelicalism had taken shape in negative reaction to the ideology of Liberal Protestantism and developed into a religion not solely of the heart but also one whose followers increasingly erected theological fences around a defensive religious "laager". As the ideology of liberal Protestantism captured the various churches, Evangelicals, particularly in Europe, chose to remain inside those churches as Low Church parties, whilst at the same time organising parallel interdenominational Evangelical networks. Paradoxically, the twentieth century spiritual descendants of the Calvins and the Wesleys are sometimes characterised by liberal perspectives which would have scandalised the progenitors of the movements. John Wesley would hardly have approved of the views of the Reverend Donald Soper nor would Professor J. Ernest Davey perhaps have found Calvin's Geneva congenial.

Although drawing on roots such as Calvinism and Wesleyanism contemporary Evangelicalism has its own specific twentieth century agenda centred, for the most part, around the inerrancy and authority of scripture and an urgency towards evangelising an ever more secularised world by dedicated and disciplined believers. The spiritual and ethical imperatives generated by these clamant demands seem to lead believers towards the same kinds of frugal and thrifty lifestyles which characterised variously the early Calvinists, the later Puritans and Methodists and render present day Evangelicals comfortable with modernity and capitalism.

Notes

1. The OMF was originally the China Inland Mission. When the Communist government expelled 600 CIM workers in 1948 they reconstituted themselves as the OMF with a remit to evangelise in Asia.

2 Interviews with Evangelical students and those from mainline backgrounds

Introduction

A central feature of the secularisation thesis has been the declining social and economic influence of religion as a consequence of the objectification of our lives through science and the march of bureaucratisation as a core element of the nation state. The Church's power to explain the events of everyday life through the agency of a supernatural being has, for the great mass of people, become something to which they give credence only at times of great emotional distress or symbolic importance. It is still felt important by many people to have a priest present and in charge at their births, weddings and death. Clergy continue to comfort the bereaved and their relatives and friends and a great many parents who would otherwise profess only a very loose set of religious beliefs and who rarely attend church services continue to seek sanctification, through baptism, for their children's lives.

These examples of the persistence of spiritual values in our lives do not, however, detract from the argument that the secularisation process has displaced the original spiritual purpose of Puritanism in the duty to dedicate social and economic life to God's glory. Such economic values are now independent of the original religious momentum which Weber argued produced them. Reference to their spiritual origins is, for the general mass of people, mostly symbolic. They retain only an allegorical significance for the secular values which determine the organisation and direction of day-to-day living. Wilson is pessimistic about this and sees it as:

> a threat to what men have meant by culture, to the constellation of artefacts, norms, values, attitudes and collective mental constructs by which men in a given society mediate their relationships and order their affairs. (Wilson, 1982, p.88.)

Such a viewpoint represents a very positive interpretation of the influence of religion in shaping a nation's values and the behaviour of its people. Historically, many would argue that it has had less wholesome effects on the intellectual development of western society. In the 16th century, for example, Copernicus's attempts to alter contemporary scientific theories of solar motion met with stiff opposition from the Catholic Church. Copernicus in 1543 had argued that the earth was merely a satellite of the sun rather than the church's view, that the earth, created in God's image, occupied the centre of the solar system with the sun and the other planets in orbit around it. By 1609, Galileo had made a telescope with which he was able to observe planetary motion directly and to confirm Copernicus's theoretical model. Unfortunately for Galileo, the Catholic counter-reformation was by then mounting a powerful campaign to re-assert the Established Church's doctrinal and intellectual authority against the mounting criticism and spread of Protestantism. Heretics were simply and mercilessly defined as those who were not wholehearted and obedient believers in the Catholic doctrine. The alternative, intellectual and religious scepticism, leading to the adoption of the new reformed faith was to attract the full weight of the church's censure through the stake or the rack as the means of 'correcting' the misguided. His subsequent trial for heresy ended in a demand for retraction of his scientific views published in his book "Dialogue in the Great World Systems". If Galileo showed any resistance, he was to be shown the instruments of torture as if they were to be used. Galileo, by then 72, recanted:

> I Galileo Galilei, ... must altogether abandon the false opinion that the sun is the centre of the world .... and that the earth is not the centre of the world and moves, and that I must not not hold, defend, or teach in any way whatsoever, verbally or in writing the said doctrine ...... the said doctrine was contrary to Holy Scripture. (Bronowski, 1976, p.216.)

He was confined to his house until his death in 1642. During this period he was forbidden to talk to Protestants and a form of strict censorship of science was introduced throughout the Mediterranean region. As a consequence the focus of scientific discovery become centred on the northern European countries, a fact which also reflected their growing economic and political power through trade and commerce across the Atlantic.

The acceptance of science and the momentum towards independent nationhood was reflected in the adoption by Puritans of a more rational form of religious beliefs than those of the established church of the time. It was less clear among contemporaries that by its nature the new religion had a powerful secularising potential. God's immanence in the world would increasingly be replaced by the laws of science and their practical application. In modern times this has resulted in a substantial decline in church membership and attendance to the extent that many lay and church observers expect religion to become a small, residual and insignificant influence to the detriment of our lives and the conduct of public affairs. This is certainly Wilson's argument:

> The implications of science for values are perhaps bleak, and the increasingly rationalised world order is one in which cultural distinctiveness may well be eliminated so to raise the question of whether in the future the condition of life will ever be wholly humane without the operation of some such [religious] agencies. (Wilson, 1982, p.88.)

Religiosity

By contrast, however, a recent survey on religious beliefs suggests that the "tide" of secularisation is not as powerful as it might appear. It suggests that about 70% of people in Great Britain believe in some form of divine being as an explanation of either their longing for, or experience of, a spiritual self (Jowell et al 1992). The finding is perhaps a reflection of the fact that important events in our lives, falling in love and marrying, close friendships, and more generally the purpose of life itself are unamenable to scientific explanation. From a more practical and politically contentious viewpoint, the churches in Latin America, for example, has been active and in the forefront of challenges to autocratic rule and the allevation of poverty through programmes of self-help which threaten dictators. This has, necessarily, brought the them into conflict with the ruling power in the countries concerned and simultaneously with their own religious authorities for going beyond their specifically religious duties. It has occurred most notably in the case of the Catholic authorities' censure of 'political' priests who take and practise too literally some of Jesus's views on the distribution of wealth, and in the Beatitudes concerning who should "inherit the earth". In Great Britain, Greeley, the author of the figures quoted here summarises British attitudes to religion as approximately 30% of Britons being not religious at all, 40% are "seriously" religious and a further 30% as being "conventionally but not seriously religious". In historical terms he suggests that:

> the British are more religious than they think they are ..... and that they are possibly more religious than they used to be. (quoted in Jowell, 1993, p.69.)

In the more politically settled and affluent context of North America there has been significant growth in the USA of literalist and fundamentalist sects over the last 10-15 years. Jerry Falwell, for example, became during the 1980's a powerful political figure through his leadership of the "moral majority" movement for the expression of conservative religious doctrines and political policies which he founded in 1980. Groups and individuals within this broad movement of the religious right have made comprehensive and skilful use of modern communication media to bring their word to the homes of believers and non-believers alike. A number of them have their own television stations used solely for preaching their views and, just as importantly, for fundraising in order that such beliefs may be more widely transmitted. The introduction of "fundamentalist" television stations has been resisted in the United Kingdom on the basis that it is perceived as "predatory" particularly in view of the misuse by a small number of such groups of funds they have raised through high powered "tele-evangelism". There is also a widespread perception in the United Kingdom, based on the activities of extreme sects such as the Unification Church, founded by the Korean Sun Myong Moon, that converts to such sects and cults will abandon their friends and parents and take up extreme lifestyles as a result of "indoctrination" by other members of the group.

That about seven tenths of adults in the UK subscribe to a belief in God does not detract from the fact of the churches' decreasing ability to influence public affairs in the economic and political management of the country and also in the regulation of the values underpinning the conduct of our everyday lives. We should, however, be careful not to presume that there was a time in the past when everyone subscribed to the church's views and that they attended obediently or that the secularisation of contemporary society has become wholly dominant. Thomas (1978) suggests that during the middle ages half-hearted devotion to Church doctrine was prevalent among the common people. He also points out that for many of the population it was not a case of accepting religion and abandoning magic, the two were to some extent symbiotic.

The ethic and spirit in late 20th century

The argument so far in this chapter has been concerned with the background to the secularisation of day-to-day life in all its various political, social and economic aspects. It is clear that few people perceive or experience the world as imbued with a supernatural or divine presence but a great number still retain some sense of religiosity, perhaps of wanting to believe in some divine purpose for their lives. In contrast with early Puritanism, Weber has observed that a mechanistic and wholly secular form of capitalism has become pre-dominant. There is, however, a variety of religious groups for whom the ethic in its original form retains a central organising principle in their lives. They have tended to follow religious beliefs and social values which run contrary to a more general secularising ethic. These are the Evangelicals of the previous chapter. They share a strong sense that God is constantly with them and that He informs and directs their daily lives in religious, social and economic spheres. The aim of the present research is to investigate how far this original sense of the calling is still alive among Evangelical students (17-20 years). Does it, for example, allow them to develop attitudes towards education and career which creates a self-fulfilling prophecy of success at both. This and other questions evolved from a common perception that Evangelical students often fulfil the stereotype of a model pupil; obedient, punctual, diligent and one who achieves good examination results. There is also a perception in Northern Ireland that Evangelical pupils proceed in large numbers to perform successfully in higher education and to enter professional and business life. This occurs against the background of a religious ethic which sets limits to followers' involvement with "worldliness". The more exclusive Brethren sects represent one end of a continuum of religious beliefs and social values which includes such features as strict dress codes, Sunday observance and the rejection of some forms of modern technology. Some exclusive Brethren children are asked by their parents to refrain from watching television in school, or videos, or using computers, on the grounds that this "worldly" technology will damage their faith and impair their witness. Most obey the parental request. The great majority of Evangelicals however would, in Bruce's term be "comfortable with modernity" (Bruce 1984); although they would still remain conservative with regard to a firm view about the moral parameters of their worldliness. Such conservatism would involve abstinence from alcohol, tobacco and a wide range of the shows, programmes and so on offered by modern entertainment media. More generally, the patterns of socialisation within the Evangelical-Baptist culture appear to develop a cluster of individualistic virtues such as frugality, thrift, self-reliance and dependability, all of which appear to be directly transferable to schooling and work.

In developing a research framework for investigating the relationship between Evangelical beliefs, educational achievement and economic success the work of Pierre Bourdieu (1977) provides a number of valuable insights. Bourdieu's central purpose is to explain the extent to which differential access to academic knowledge, educational success at school and cultural processes form the ideational structure through which social and economic stratification is reproduced. Schooling, he suggests, is the essential agent for the transmission of a class-based culture by representing both the process of schooling as impartial and the knowledge structure, the curriculum, as the ideal. This is based on the assumption that it embodies universally agreed principles and qualities on which the continuation of our way of life, the culture, is premissed. These he defines collectively as "intellectual fields". Ownership of these he argues leads to domination of the chief pathways to educational and economic success

Access to these "fields" is crucial, Bourdieu argues, in helping individuals to understand the principles of their culture and in how to use them to inform their behaviour and to achieve success at education and work in their society. But there is differential access to and understanding of the intellectual "fields" determined largely, he argues, by social class. Those from professional and managerial backgrounds experience a continuity of expectations, language and behaviour, between home and school. With respect to the curriculum, pupils from such homes develop what Bourdieu describes as an "aristocratic" attitude toward it in the extent to which they expect intellectual progress and success whereas pupils from manual backgrounds encounter schooling in terms of discontinuity with their backgrounds. The result, he argues, is that the latter under-achieve as measured by success at examinations and access to higher education and its accompanying entrée into the industry and professions.

In this way, existing hierarchies of employment prospects and, more generally, life-chances are preserved or in Bourdieu's view, culturally reproduced, especially through the agency of the family and school. Children from backgrounds of higher status and income "inherit" from their parents the social and intellectual attributes central to educational success. Two features of this process are relevant to the present analysis of the views of Evangelical and Mainline religious pupils. The first is acquisition by pupils of what Bourdieu calls "cultural capital" which is acquired from family life and gives individuals the essential foundation for learning social and linguistic competences crucial for success at school. It also enables them to develop confidence about their culture and an expectation of educational achievement and future career success. Working class pupils, in general, Bourdieu argues, do not have a similar form of cultural capital and have a less positive disposition towards school culture than their middle-class counterparts. Class differences, he argues, can be most clearly measured in the extent to which the cultural capital as experienced in the home is distinct from the school and, at school, the experience of academic and everyday knowledge as separate and discrete entities.

Following this analysis, Evangelicals would be expected to assimilate a strongly religious form of cultural capital. This would give them "master patterns" through which they can judge the legitimacy, according to their beliefs, of certain forms of behaviour, belief and social practices.

Overall, Evangelicals establish a relationship to the world which is constructed from and legitimised chiefly by scripture. In its strongest form this is based on an inerrantist approach to the Bible, that it is the revealed word of God and therefore literally true and correct. In this context, Bourdieu could have had the present research in mind when he argued:

> it (school and family) is obliged to establish and define systematically the sphere of orthodox culture and the sphere of heretical culture. Simultaneously, it defends consecrated culture against the continued challenge offered by the mere existence of new creators ..... who can arouse

in the public (and particularly in the intellectual classes) new demands and rebellious doubts. (Bourdieu, 1971, p.178.)

The argument here is that the cultural capital acquired by Evangelical students enables them to distinguish on theological and moral grounds between "consecrated" and "heretical" culture. The criteria for acceptability are an integral part of Bourdieu's idea of the "habitus" which each person, religious and non-religious alike, acquires as part of the process of socialisation within the family. Through the conscious and unconscious processes of learning about culture in all its variety of representation we develop a structure of perceptions and thought concerning the world. Bourdieu suggests that:

> the principles embodied in this way are placed beyond the grasp of consciousness, and hence cannot be touched by voluntary, deliberate transformation, cannot even be made explicit ...... (Bourdieu, 1990, pp.93-94.)

For Evangelicals this would result in the creation of a common consciousness whose theological parameters would be set by reference to study of texts such as W. E. Vine's "Bible Dictionary" or "The Tyndale Commentaries" in addition to the Bible itself. Socially, behaviour would be thinkable or otherwise according to the patterns of deep structural social and ethical dispositions towards worldliness which had been built-up over generations within Evangelical communities.

It is possible that an Evangelical home, therefore, gives children a "habitus" from which students are able to develop a social and moral grammar that filters aspects of "worldliness" with respect to their usefulness, acceptability, suitability and so on. In the present context, the argument is that it also gives them a particular orientation towards education and career which is positive in both attitude and expectation of success. They come to school with a "habitus" developed within the family which gives them the attitudes, value and skills necessary for academic progress in school.

The hypothesis as to Evangelical pupils' approach to learning and progress at school are also "grounded" in teachers' perceptions of pupils from Evangelical backgrounds. These, in fact, in bio-data terms, have sometimes unpromising with respect to indicators such as family wealth, few relatives or family members having gone on to higher education, or having been employed in professional, and academic careers or having achieved powerful and highly rewarded positions in business. Yet in preliminary discussions with teachers and others a clear impression emerged that Evangelicals' family and church backgrounds instilled in them high levels of motivation to achieve. It was also argued, with respect to the skills required at school, that their commitment to and habits of studying the Bible and the approved Bible concordances and commentaries gave such pupils a headstart. Linguistic skills were highlighted as a consequence of such study and similarly music was also perceived as a particular strength of Evangelical pupils, probably, it was argued, because of its prominence in worship and para-church social activities. The nature of their religious beliefs might also be expected to promote habits of obedience and conformity to school authority structures to the extent that teachers, from initial discussions with them about the research project, perceived Evangelicals as 'model' or 'ideal' pupils.

For research purposes a group of hypotheses concerning Evangelical beliefs, patterns of family life and intellectual skills based on biblical study has emerged: the underlying theme is that these non-school elements transfer to future educational and vocational success. In turning these into practical but 'grounded' research questions, Glaser & Strauss caution against the "opportunistic use of theory" through what they call "exampling" where:

> A researcher can easily find examples for dreamed-up, speculative, or logically deduced theory after the idea has occurred. .....Therefore, one receives the image of a proof when there is none, and the theory obtains a richness of detail that it did not earn. (Glaser and Straus, 1967, p.5.)

They do not argue that researchers should let the data "tell their own story", however, but suggest that adherence to a particular theory presumes a confirmatory (for the theory) framework for the selection of research questions and examples chosen from any subsequent data.

By contrast, they suggest that:

> grounded theory can be presented either as a well-codified set of propositions or in running theoretical discussion .... The form in which a theory is presented does not make a theory; it is a theory because it explains or predicts something. (p.31.)

In the case of the present research the "running theoretical discussion" was adopted as the procedure for both collecting and analysing data.

Analysis of the interviews

Cohen & Manion (1989) describe four types of interview which are most frequently used in educational and other social science research. The first these is the structured interview where questions are pre-set and for all practical purposes are the same as postal type questionnaire items but where responses are recorded face-to-face. The second is the unstructured interview where there is greater freedom for both participants to phrase and interpret questions. Although the interviewer will have in mind the general direction of the questioning, the interviewee can open up areas not initially considered. A third type is the non-directive interview closely resembles the psycho-analytical model where respondents are encouraged in "free association" to express their feelings and attitudes. The interviewer imposes only a very loose form of control over the process and is confined to re-interpreting and probing into responses given by the interviewee. The fourth type is described by Cohen & Manion as the 'focused interview' which is a firmer and more strongly determined version than the unstructured type of interview. In this case the interviewer concentrates on a number of prepared "domain issues" to be put to all interviewees. Each is usually accompanied by a set of subsidiary "probes" which can be used to elicit responses if there is misunderstanding about a particular issue or to develop greater depth of discussion. Using this type of interview gives greater scope for an in-depth dialogue between participants while simultaneously enabling the interviewer to retain control over the direction and any potential subjective "drift" of the interview.

This last type of interview was employed in the present research. It enabled us to investigate in depth attitudes and values about questions such as interviewees' religious beliefs and their relationship to school and choice of future career whilst also allowing us to articulate our own concepts in the form of "domain issues". In Glaser & Straus's terms it was an attempt to develop "a running theoretical discussion" with the data as it evolved from the pupils' interviews. The adoption of an overall ethnographic approach is based on the argument that whilst it is impossible ever to enter another's consciousness we can nevertheless come close to understanding their behaviour by examining how and why they give meaning to their actions. Interview techniques are a natural extension of this view because of the way in which meaning and understanding are mediated and constructed through language. Interest in the interview then focuses in the case of the present research on the way in which student's subjective meanings interact with the objective world of school, career, family and so on. This methodology owes much to the work of G. M. Mead (1934) in "Mind, Self and Society" and the school of sociological theory and research which became known as "Symbolic Interaction", one of whose central ideas concerns the essential social nature of constructing meanings where we "take the role of the other". On this basis, it is argued, we imaginatively assemble and play through the reactions and behaviour of others to our own ideas and intended actions. Reality, in this sense, becomes a process of negotiation where we reflect upon and change our actions according to our construction of other people's potential reaction to our own behaviour and plans. Reality, it is argued, is much more permeable and tentative than we normally assume.

Another form of this broadly qualitative approach enjoins the researcher to take nothing for granted and to become absolved of all personal pre-conceptions about the research subject. This perspective is called social phenomenology and one of its founders Alfred Schutz (1962, p.64 & 66) raises the possibility of bridging the gap between subject and object or interviewee and researcher which remains a core problem for any research which attempts to go beyond the outward representation through, for example, questionnaires of values and attitudes. This is also expressed more generally in the philosophy of the social sciences as problems concerning holistic and individualist explanations of behaviour, the extent to which we can talk of ourselves as acting voluntarily or having our actions largely determined by, for example, our gender, race, class or in this case religious beliefs. For Schutz and later writers in this tradition the purpose of research should be to come as close as possible to the "natural attitude" by stripping away the subject's taken-for-granted assumptions, or what Schutz called "typifications". These are based on where we grow up and the way we create attitudes to others generated by the more general pre-suppostions about gender, race and social class which we encounter in the objective world we live in. We each develop, it is argued, an individual subjective interpretation or accommodation to that reality. By reflecting on these subjectivities through research interviews we can gain a picture of how they inter-relate. The "life-world" and "intentionalities" can be revealed as a means of explaining how each person acts and develops attitudes towards others.

In the case of the present research the interviews were focused on the students' "life-world" with respect to the interaction between the subjective world of Evangelicals' religious beliefs and the objective reality of a secular world with different moral and social values. This was investigated through the discussion of a number of "domain issues" which related to core aspects of Evangelical beliefs, social values, worship and attitudes towards school and future career choices. At the same time, the interviews were designed to explore the nature of the cognitive "map" which Evangelicals developed on the basis of their family background. The hypothesis was that, as a result of bible study and discussion of interpretation from commentaries and other Evangelical literature, students from such backgrounds would be able to convert this "cultural capital" into success at curricular subjects with a core language component such as modern languages, English and history. In a similar way it was thought that the scripturally based moral discipline of the family and the wider Evangelical community would impart a "habitus" to students from that background which had at its core an expectation of success at school and, later on, the extent to which religious beliefs influenced students when choosing a career. Did they see this choice, for example, in the context of "God's Will"? A comparative approach to the investigation was also included in the research by arranging a similar set of interviews with students from what were defined as "Mainline" religious backgrounds including Presbyterians, Methodists, Church of Ireland (Anglican) and Roman Catholics. These students were asked the same type of questions as the Evangelical sample. This approach enabled us to bring the Evangelical moral and cognitive "maps" into sharper focus by analysing their beliefs and skills alongside those of students who had firm religious beliefs but who did not see themselves as being Evangelical as the term would be normally defined.

This presented an important initial difficulty in recruiting samples of both types of student for interview. A common stereotypical perception of Evangelicalism in Northern Ireland, with regard to organised religious groups, would centre around those from Baptist, Pentecostals and Brethren backgrounds. Among their beliefs the idea of being "saved" complemented by adult baptism and an ethic of separation from certain aspects of "worldliness" would generally be regarded as core features of their beliefs and religious practice. Originally, in order to obtain a clear research focus, it had been intended to recruit Evangelicals of this general Baptist type. However, in the context of Glaser & Strauss's injunction to create a "running theoretical discussion with the data", Evangelicalism was understood as inclusive of Anglican, Presbyterian, Methodist and Roman Catholic students because of their insistence during the preliminary phase of the research that their Evangelical "credentials" were as solid as those from a general Baptist background.

The most practicable definition of Evangelical beliefs revolved around the Wesleyan idea of assurance as expressed in the hymn:

Blessed assurance, Jesus is mine

O what a foretaste of glory divine.

This meant that Evangelical interviewees were chosen on the basis of their certainty of religious belief allied with a strict adherence to their practice through regular church attendance both on Sundays and other mid-week activities such as bible-study classes, fellowship meetings or sacred music practices. The underlying and distinguishing feature of the Evangelical sample was a religious ethic of certainty.

As a further refinement of the process of selecting the samples a set of typical answers to questions about beliefs allowed us to designate individuals as Evangelical rather than Mainline. This was carried our during a preliminary discussion with all potential interviewees. Responses such as:

I am born again.

I have experienced the new birth.

I know that my sins are forgiven and that I am going to heaven.

I have a personal experience of the Lord Jesus.

or a quotation such as:

You ask me how I know He lives, He lives within my heart.

were also used to distinguish between Evangelical and Mainline students.

Other indicators included such prominent features of the present day Evangelical world as readership of books and other material from the Inter-varsity Press, the Tyndale Press and from Bible Colleges such as London and the Fuller Bible College, Pasadena, USA. Membership of the Universities and Colleges Christian Fellowship and in schools of the Scripture Union Movement is a definitive indicator.

The criteria for recruiting the Mainline sample involved a similar discussion which revolved around holding definite religious beliefs but not in the Evangelical sense of being unquestionably certain about them. Church attendance was also used as an indicator but Mainline students were defined as taking a more relaxed attitude to religious practice. For sampling purposes the definition did not extend, however, to those whose attendance was in any real sense episodic or arbitrary.

Interview analysis: Biographical data

A total of 40 interviews were drawn from a larger corpus of 60 interviews; these were 20 Evangelical students and 20 from Mainline religious backgrounds. The criterion for selection was chiefly the quantity of response data. A considerable number of Evangelical interviews yielded very little analyseable data; this was especially the case with girls from working class backgrounds who attended Pentecostal churches. On the Mainline side, there were a number of respondents who were shy and unforthcoming and who gave little by way of data. There were others from the same background whose religious practice turned out to be overly fragmented or episodic and who could not, therefore, be used as comparators. Some high school pupils and undergraduates were interviewed in North America but owing to educational differences the data could only be used impressionistically. The sample broke down as follows:

Qualitative Semi-structured Interviews

Sample	Evangelical (20)	Control (20) interviews
	1 Roman Catholic	6 Roman Catholic
	3 Brethren	5 Church of Ireland
	4 Baptist	9 Presbyterian
	4 Elim	
	3 Church of Ireland	
	4 Presbyterian	
	1 Methodist	

Career choice

Both sets of interviewees were asked about their future career preferences and the following pattern emerged:

Evangelical Sample		Mainline Sample	
Theological	2	Business	1
Teaching	4	Teaching	5
Social Worker	2	Social Worker	2
Medicine	2	Medicine	2
Law	3	Dentist	1
Engineering	2	Travel Industry	1
Biochemistry	1	Chemist	1
Music	1	Languages	2
Journalism	1	Dentist	1
Air Traffic Control	1	America	1
Year out	1	No choice yet	3
(3 going to Cambridge)		(1 going to Cambridge)	

Fourteen per cent of the Evangelical sample saw their choice of future career as being strongly influenced by God. Their choice was perceived as a vocation in the strong sense of being "called" to a particular occupation. This was most strongly felt in the case of students who intended to go on to medicine, teaching, social work, theology and, in the case of one A level student, civil engineering, which he saw both as a career and means of carrying out missionary work:

> I would perhaps do civil engineering and do some missionary work.

Another student expressed a similar viewpoint:

> After I qualify as a doctor I would like to go away, possibly to India or some Third World country and work there for a while.

When asked further about the spiritual reasons for "aiming high" in choosing a career this same student replied:

> Yes I think work is one of the things that I can be good at and I think it is a way of worshipping if I do it to the best of my ability.

By contrast, four of the group felt that career choice would be influenced by a sense of carrying out "God's will":

> I feel there has been a reason for getting a good education 'all things come together for good for those who love the Lord' and I think everything is planned.

Another more typical response:

> There would be a spiritual element —— I'm just taking it step by step.

For the Evangelical students, career choice is closely related to their perception of God's purpose for their working lives. This is most clearly expressed in the context of service, with medicine, teaching, social work, missionary work and in one case civil engineering emerging as choices aligned with a sense of divine direction and purpose. Responses to questions about future career choice give some support to the idea of what Weber thought of as a "calling" which combines spiritual and secular values. It is arguable that there is some continuity with early Protestants' "worldly asceticism" with regard to modern Evangelical students' reasons for choosing a career in so far as spiritual values appear to be pre-eminent whilst they also recognise the value in secular terms of "a good job" and the prestige of a professional career.

Family and personal bible study

The purpose of questions concerning bible study was to explore how far students felt it benefitted them in academic work rather than as a measure of how devout they were. Questions were directed toward students' bible reading practice as a learning experience in so far as it helped them to develop skills of textual analysis and interpretation. Interviewees were also asked to what extent they felt that studying the Bible at home, either as a family or individually, helped them at school with subjects such as English, history, geography, languages and music.

From the interview data none of the students in either group set time aside for family Bible reading, although 18 (90%) Evangelical students had a set period during the day for personal prayer and private Bible study. This applied to only 6 (30%) of the control sample. The absence of family Bible reading appeared to be related to the age of the students who were in the 17-21 age range with parents abandoning it after a certain age:

Question:

> Do you have family Bible readings?

Answer:

> Not any more, we used to have when we were younger but I think my parents feel that we are old enough now to read for ourselves. (Evangelical Student)

Another said:

> There would have been (Bible study) when I was younger but now that I
> am older I wouldn't spend too much time in the house. (Evangelical student)

With regard to individual approaches to scripture study guides such as "Everyday
with Jesus", other commentaries and study aids of the type of Vine's Bible
dictionary appeared to be a popular way of helping to read and interpret biblical
passages:

> My father has Cruden's Concordance which I would use if required. I also
> use a handbook of the Bible which gives me a good background to cultural
> tradition. I'm not best at Bible reading but I'm taking a Bible course and it
> looks at the different books written about the Bible from a number of aspects.
> (Evangelical Student)

Mainline students viewpoints were summed up by one student who commented:

> I certainly say prayers at night but I don't have to read the Bible.

The social world and the church

On average Evangelical students were spending 10 hours per week on worship
and other church related activities. By contrast, the Mainline group reported an
average of 2 hours devoted to the church. When not given over to specific
periods of worship, Evangelical students are active in a wide range of activities
nearly all of which are focussed on church organisations such as the Girls' Brigade
Fellowship meetings and church music:

> I am a member of the Tear Fund Committee (at school). (Evangelical
> student)

> I've been in the Girls' Brigade since I was 2 years old, every Tuesday night
> from 7.30 to 10.30....and on Saturday night I go to the Youth Club.
> (Evangelical student)

> I used to go to Sunday School and Bible Class, now I take Sunday School
> (Evangelical student)

Most of the Mainline students were more distanced from the church in their
social activities. Academic study was a clear priority for many who were
preparing for A levels or university examinations:

41

I go to church on Sundays but I have little time for any thing else as I am studying for A levels. (Mainline student)

Music also emerged as a prominent feature of Evangelical social life and clearly provided a valued opportunity for fellowship with other members of their church:

in the Youth Group there are 4 or 5 of us that play musical instruments, so occasionally we would get together and prepare something for a church service and once every so often we would take a whole service ... (Evangelical student)

The idea of fellowship extends more widely to other social interaction and gives a clear picture of the interpretation of religious beliefs and social behaviour:

there is a very active youth group in my church which I belong to. We are quite a social group, we tend to go out bowling together or out for a meal together, —— as well as on Sunday nights whatever programme the leaders have planned, we follow. (Evangelical student)

There is the Youth Fellowship in the church and the Bible Union and Christian Union here (in school). (Evangelical student)

Mainline students tended to keep their social lives separate from church to a greater extent, often claiming pressure of time or plain lack of interest:

"I used to be a Sunday School teacher 2 years ago for six or seven months in the Methodist church. I would like to do it again but I have so much other schoolwork at the minute".

For Evangelical students there were, however, well prescribed parameters for social activities based on their religious beliefs. These were used to interpret or gauge the acceptability of common social and entertainment pastimes such as discos, the cinema, the theatre and holidays. One Evangelical student gave a clear idea of how this works and shapes her attitudes towards invitations to accompany friends to plays, discos and acceptable music:

I like gospel tapes - Graham Kendrick, Amy Grant. I disagree with Amy Grant in that she is now producing more worldly songs and is in the charts.

Interviewer:

Would you feel happy about going to the cinema or disco with them? (non-Evangelical friends)

Student:

No I wouldn't, I would feel uneasy about it, because I know they would want to go somewhere after it and I would feel quite uneasy about that.

Interviewer:

What about discos?

Student: I totally disagree with them.

Interviewer:

What kind of places would you go to with friends from Church?

Student:

Bowling —— or go out for something to eat or to a friend's house. (Evangelical student)

Another Evangelical student was quite explicit in deciding about entertainment and other social activities:

I know the difference between right and wrong and morals. I know the church would always be there for me and would help and pray for me if I needed help in any way.

Mainline responses ranged from "Heavy Metal", "Pop Music" to a mixture of popular and Christian music with little impression of certain types of music being "ring-fenced" as "unsuitable" in terms of them running contrary to their religious beliefs. Evangelical students appear to have developed from their family and church values which enable them to be 'in the world", to be ambitious, diligent in their school and aiming for prestigious and well rewarded careers. At the same time, however, they seem to separate those aspects of worldliness which, for them, have a sound and proper moral and religious purpose, from others which are contrary to their beliefs and values. The latter attitudes towards entertainment and a variety of social activities resonate with early Protestants' rejection of the traditional accompaniments of wealth and success: what they saw as "sins of the flesh". There remains among this sample of Evangelical students and their families a clear though less restrictive set of operational principles which help them both to be "comfortable with modernity" and to remain separate from what they view as its unsuitable aspects.

With regard to "worldly" entertainment both groups were asked about the presence and control of television, videos and radio in their homes. The differences between the two samples in this respect are minimal which is perhaps unexpected given the pervasiveness and scope of the media and the wide variety of acceptability of programmes available. When asked further about their use both groups of students held similar views with respect to programmes which they would watch:

There would be control (on programmes) to a certain extent. There would be programmes that my parents would not wish the family to watch.

Interviewer:

Would you control the TV yourself at all, saying 'you are 18'?

Student:

Yes I wouldn't want to watch things that wouldn't be good for my faith. (Mainline student)

An Evangelical student commented:

I never really watched a lot of TV but when I was younger after a certain time I wouldn't have been allowed to watch TV. If there was a new programme they (parents) would have watched it with me.

Another student said:

With regard to the type of programme we could watch, Mum would try to censor things and she would read up on what things are about. (Evangelical student)

The interviews suggest that the families of both groups of students take a benign approach to TV, video and radio with regard to their acceptability in the home. There are some differences in the restrictions placed on use with Evangelical parents and their children themselves exercising greater control over programmes in terms of them offending or undermining their religious beliefs and values. These views are consistent with Evangelical students' attitudes towards entertainment outside the home, such as discos, cinema, theatre, sport, concerts and so on. These are are either acceptable or unacceptable according to whether or not they breach a combined pattern of social and religious values which have been developed within Evangelical families. Students from Mainline religious backgrounds are subject to similar controls on their viewing and listening habits. The main differences appear to be a somewhat more liberal application of what is acceptable in Mainline homes.

Motivation

Both groups were asked about the sorts of values which they relied on to motivate them towards success at school and elsewhere. The questions were designed to build up a picture of what Bourdieu calls a "habitus"; a set of attitudes and habits of work which pre-dispose some students to an expectation of success at school and others to pessimism or indifference towards it. In Bourdieu's case these orientations to schoolwork largely follow social class lines. In the present research, by contrast, the concentration was placed upon the extent to which religious beliefs provide the inspiration for doing well at school and the pursuit of a future successful career. Both sets of students received support and encouragement from their parents which is perhaps not unusual given the overall ability and background of the interviewees (Lower VIth form and 1st year university). The chief difference appears to lie in a closer involvement and monitoring of their children's schoolwork by Evangelical parents and a sense that academic achievement was an extension of a general pattern of belief and worship for Evangelical students:

Interviewer:

> Where would you place most credit on your academic achievements to date?

Student:

> It's got to be a mixture......parental support has been valuable, support from my church, spiritual background - I don't think I would have got through a lot of exams without prayer. If it wasn't God's will I don't think I would be happy in what I would be doing. (Evangelical student)

Another Evangelical student replied:

> I feel that God has given you certain gifts and I feel that you should use them for His glory.

When asked about motivation for success at school Mainline students tended to place less emphasis on religious values as their main source of motivation:

> I just like to do well. Mum and dad have done so much for me I would like to do well and please them. Plus I would like to do well for myself. To please my parents and myself. I don't really worry about exams, just worry if I fail them what would I do?.

Mainline and Evangelicals alike in the present sample are clearly ambitious at school and expect to be successful at academic work.

It is clear from the interviews that there is a strong degree of continuity between family and school "habitus". This is characterised by an expectation of academic achievement to be followed by future career success. Evangelical students can be distinguished from Mainline students by reference to the strongly scriptural basis of their family values. Attitudes to study appear to be closely mirrored by the family's approach to academic work and worship. In a sense, these would seem difficult to separate in Evangelical homes where religious purposes underpin all aspects of family life and work and school outside it.

Conclusion

Analysis of the interviews offers insight into both groups of students' religious beliefs and the way in which these affect their values concerning academic success, social behaviour, entertainment and future career choice. Evangelical students' interviews also offer viewpoints which run contrary to the "tide of secularism" with regard to the social "rules" which govern their engagement with the world. In choosing a career, for example, their religious beliefs provide a powerful context which affords clear criteria of acceptability. These include a 20th century interpretation of the earlier Protestant idea of a "calling", that a career should be considered on the grounds of being as part of God's purpose for each person. This was often represented as service through careers such as medicine, social work, law, teaching and in more directly religious careers. There was no suggestion, however, from any of the interviewees from either of the groups that the choice of a prestigious and highly paid career was in any way at variance with their religious beliefs. The Evangelical students were, as a whole, highly motivated towards achieving a career that was both spiritually and materially rewarding. There is little evidence that such choices and their rewards were perceived by Evangelicals as a way of demonstrating their moral or religious superiority over others who did not hold such beliefs. Neither was worldly success interpreted as a token of suitability for life beyond the here and now.

Present day Evangelical students' religious beliefs appear to provide them with an underlying moral grammar for answering questions and dilemmas about their involvement with the world. This sets limits on their social behaviour and interaction with others of their own age where "heavy" discos, "adult" cinema, and so on are ruled out because of the perceived offence they give to Evangelicals' ideas of spirituality. This feeling was strongly expressed during the interviews in terms of a clear distinction between "right" and "wrong" - that, as one Evangelical student said:

I know that my religion will always be there for me.

This was said with reference to making decisions as to social behaviour and invitations to parties and discos. This disengagement from widely acceptable worldly entertainment places the religious community of the church at the centre of social life. Music, for example, provided an important focus for meeting and creating entertainment in the company of other co-religionists with shared views concerning the spiritual basis of their enjoyment in practising and performing music. Bible study classes have a similar dual purpose often expressed as "fellowship". For Evangelicals this means something much more than "being in the company of" :   it is reserved, in this context, for others of similar beliefs and obviates the need for raising questions of acceptability of, for example, types of music, forms of entertainment and subjects for discussions or conversation. For many Evangelical students, church and social life appear to be indistinguishable although in the case of the present interviewees this was not perceived as a retreat from the world. Many of them were involved in worthwhile community work and with Third World charities.

In discussing educational aims and achievements it was also evident that Evangelical students were clearly focussed on academic success which, although important in its own right, was also perceived as the means of attaining a career which embodied status, service and a good salary. In managing both of these aims Evangelical students came from a background or what Bourdieu calls a "habitus" where there is a strong expectation of diligence and success. This appeared to cross social class boundaries with regard to interviews with students who came from working class backgrounds, a number of whom were first generation 'A' level or university students. There was a clear sense of continuity between values expressed at home and at school with the added factor, in the case of Evangelical students, that there was a primary spiritual purpose to their pursuit of academic success. In terms of specific habits of study there was no clear picture that skills acquired through Bible study could be directly applied to school subjects. There was little suggestion from interviewees that the study of Bible Concordances and commentaries was perceived as other than scripturally conceived.

3 Analysis of survey data

From a methodological viewpoint the analysis of Evangelical students' religious, educational and social milieu has so far been based on qualitative research perspectives. Although there are different emphases among qualitative researchers, their approaches would nevertheless be centrally concerned with the individual's subjective experience of the world in creating a social reality. In terms of the theory underpinning such an approach it presumes a voluntaristic perspective on our role in creating the social world around us; that we are not merely social "products" determined by an external reality but retain the ability to create and modify that reality. With regard to social science research such a view, taken to extreme, has led to explanations which methodologically exclude any reference to general or universalisable research findings by concentrating upon what is unique and distinct to each person. Explanations are essentially *from within*. An example would be the way in which social phenomenological research challenges accepted social reality by questioning our taken-for-granted assumptions about everyday life. These are the ground rules which, it is argued, enable us to make sense of the differing social "arenas" we encounter and to subjectively interpret worlds such as work, home and leisure. Particular examples of this approach were pioneered in the ethnomethodological perspective of Harold Garfinkel where in one famous experiment students were asked to behave almost as strangers in their own homes and to take nothing for granted in their relationships with other members of the family. This not only revealed the vital areas of unspoken consensus and rules governing family life but also threatened to undermine it in the process of revealing them. More generally qualitative researchers would argue that because of the confusion and uncertainty of everyday life we necessarily must take many aspects of it for granted. They then become embedded in our consciousness and lead to "typified", routine approaches to social reality where through time we perceive our behaviour in the context merely of reactions to the external world.

In the previous chapter a qualitative approach was adopted because of its appropriateness in explaining "from within" how Evangelical and Mainline students' religious beliefs affect their attitudes to school, future career and social and family life. The chief research tool was in-depth interviews through which the subjects' academic, religious, social and moral outlooks were probed and their inter-relationships made apparent. In the course of these it became evident that on their own the interviews would not provide a fully adequate explanation concerning questions about the two groups' attitudes and motivation towards academic success, "worldliness" and its material rewards.

This view relates to the argument raised earlier about the nature of social reality and the extent to which external social and economic entities influence our lives. We know, for example, that social class remains a significant determinant of our expectations of health and economic prospects. This is similarly the case with regard to gender where it has a significant effect on career patterns and more general cultural stereotypes concerning men and women's behaviour, sexuality, and at school, the subjects which pupils typically choose, especially at 'A' level and in higher education (17+) where fewer girls take up maths and physical sciences.

In the present research it was clear during the course of the interviews that for Evangelical students especially the church, denomination or sect[1] to which a student belonged became a significant reference point when responding to questions or discussing the impact of their particular beliefs. The student who said "I know that my religion would always be there for me ..." when deciding upon the acceptability of different types of social activities and behaviour is a clear case of the influence of an external organisation, her church, on her behaviour.

It is equally the case that when choosing a future career a significant number of Evangelical students see their choice against the backgrounds of their religious beliefs, through the emphasis on service and "God's will". At the same time, they are also aware of the prestige and material rewards of their choices and see no conflict with their beliefs and attaining "worldly" success. In both cases the external agencies of church and occupational structure interact with and impinge upon subjective reality when choices are being considered.

Following earlier arguments from Glaser and Strauss concerning the importance of "grounding" theory in the actual life experience of people, the research set out in this chapter complements the qualitative approach of the previous chapter by adopting more quantitative techniques.

An attempt was made to combine both subject and object by reference to students' inner religious ontologies and their experiences of and the extent to which they are shaped by external realities concerning school, family and future career choices. The chief research tool used was a postal questionnaire derived from the interview data, in such a way as to explain both groups of students' behaviour in terms of their interaction with parents, (Bourdieu) teachers, other students, their attitudes to study and the parameters of their social and moral realities.

From the interviews 30 statements were compiled each having an Evangelical and a more liberal Mainline "pole". (see Appendix 2) In effect, this resulted in 30 positive and 30 negative statements with responses recorded on a scale ranging from 5 to 1. A coding of 5 and 4 on the scale represented a commitment to the Evangelical pole while 1 and 2 corresponded to a more liberal Mainline pole. A score of 3 was coded as indeterminate. The questionnaire was distributed to 350 available students from Evangelical and Mainline backgrounds who were willing to participate. These included membership of groups such as school and university based Bible Unions, the Student Christian Movement and other religious societies. The age range was from 17 (6th form students at school) to 20 years (1st and 2nd year university). The attitude scale was preceded by an inventory of biographical questions related to age, gender, occupation and education of parents. Other questions were also concerned with religious beliefs and were used to determine whether respondents were either Evangelical or Mainline in their beliefs as they were described in chapter 3. Information was also sought on their current level of academic attainment chiefly with respect to GCSE and A level results and future career choice.

61.7 per cent (216) of the sample returned useable questionnaires, 96 were designated as Evangelical and 120 as coming from Mainline religious backgrounds. Statistical analysis (SPSS) revealed that 10 of the original items were insufficiently discriminating and were eliminated from any further analysis. The mean age of the sample was 17.78 years.

Religious beliefs and academic values

The attitude survey revealed that the two groups differed significantly in their responses to 13 of the questionnaire items; all but three were greater than the 0.001 level of significance.[2] The first item of the questionnaire concerned the relationship between "involvement with church" and as a result "feeling a better person". The Evangelical group, not unexpectedly, saw a close relationship with their church as a benefit in their personal values. The Mainline group were much less certain ($p = 0.000$). The next item (4) revolved around co-operative and individualist values. Non-Evangelical students as a group reported themselves as enjoying "helping other students with school/university work" to a greater extent ($p = 0.000$) than Evangelical students who believed "one should be solely responsible for one's own work". The Evangelical viewpoint here chimes in with a more general ethic of self-reliance within such groups or perhaps the view that helping others is more tightly defined with reference to the needs of members of their own group perceived as taking priority over the requirements of others outside the assembly of co-religionists. Perhaps there is a resonance in this respect to the New Testament; Jesus in the gospels teaches love of neighbour and prayer for one's enemies. The Pauline and Petrine and Johannine epistles lay more stress on love and concern for the christian fellowship

Views about linking bible study with academic competence items differed widely among Evangelical and Mainline students; the mean scores on this item were respectively 3.6 and 1.8 (p = <0.000). Whilst to some extent this result was again not unexpected, it nevertheless points to a defining difference between the two groups in their approaches to schoolwork. This is echoed in another item (11) where Evangelicals were "confident that I will do well because I trust that God will bless my efforts" whereas Mainline students feel that "my success in academic achievements is not influenced by my belief in God". (p = <0.000). The findings concerning the basis for academic values are consistent with those relating to moral principles. Mainline students believe that "morality and personal goodness can be achieved even without any religious belief" (14). Evangelicals differ (p < 0.000) believing that Christian teaching is the only way that one can be "morally upright". Whilst attitudes on this issue may be expected to differ, given the separateness of Evangelicals' beliefs, they are not as exclusive as at first sight it might appear. The mean scores are significantly different, but with a mean of 3.31 the Evangelical viewpoint is nearer the indeterminate measure than a more narrowly-focused score in the 4-5 range which might have been expected. By contrast, the Mainline score of 1.93 shows clearly the group's openness towards the source and application of moral principles.

With respect to career choice there was a clear divergence in relation to choosing or aspiring to a job which was perceived as being "in line with God's will" (15). Evangelicals' motivation was strongly rooted in this principle whilst Mainline students were more likely to have "never really considered a career in line with God's will". These respective views are reflected in the samples' attribution of academic success where Evangelicals felt that God's help was an important factor in performing well at school (16) whereas Mainline students saw achievement in a more secular and individualist context (p < 0.000). With regard to Weber's idea that the early Puritans held a "this-worldly asceticism", the Evangelical sample clearly have a keener appreciation of the relationships between academic attainment and the ability to "pursue a successful, well-paid job" than the Mainline group (p < 0.000) who feel more disposed towards the view that "worldly success is not particularly important" (18).

The relationship between conscientiousness and religious belief (19) was also examined and responses are significantly different ($p < 0.000$) with Evangelical students focusing more clearly on their religious beliefs as the basis of conscience than the Mainline sample although both means, 2.98 and 2.16 respectively, are on the non-Evangelical more secularized, liberal side of the scale. Any ambivalence, however, about achievement motivation is resolved in a later item (20) where Evangelicals "want to succeed in life in order to please God" in contrast to the Mainline sample for whom success is to be measured in so far as it benefits "myself and my family" ($p < 0.000$).

The two samples also differed on three other items but at a lesser level of significance ($p < 0.05$). Firstly, responses show the Mainline sample as more collaborative in working with other students than Evangelical students who "always prefer to work things out for my self". Secondly, Evangelicals appear to have a stronger sense of separateness because of their beliefs. They were more in line with the view that "My particular beliefs set me apart from the other students and their lifestyle" (12). Mainline students, although professing a firm faith, did not have as strong a separatist ethic. It is noteworthy, however, that both groups' means are towards the non-Evangelical part of the scale and therefore, in the case of the Evangelicals, less exclusive than they might at first sight appear. Lastly, both groups appear to be willing followers of school rules, although Evangelical students appear to be more in tune with the formal aspects of school life than the Mainline sample (13).

Academic outcomes

When attitudes are aligned with academic outcomes among the present samples it is clear that one commonly held perception of Evangelicals as model pupils and above average achievers is somewhat more complex than it might appear. GCSE and A-level results were recorded on the questionnaire as part of a range of biographical information and a rating scale applied to the results as they were given to us. Since the sample was drawn from selectivegrammar school 6th forms and higher education students, only GCSE passes at C or above were recorded; the scale used was A = 3, B = 2, C = 1. The results show a clear linguistic bias towards Evangelical students at age 16 (GCSE). They were performing significantly better in French, ($p < 0.000$), geography ($p < 0.05$), R.E ($p < 0.001$), English Literature (0.05) and English Language ($p < 0.05$). In terms of the conceptual aims of the project there is some evidence here of what Bourdieu calls "cultural capital" in relation to the emphasis among Evangelicals on daily Bible reading and frequent reading and discussion of missionary literature. It is arguable that there is some degree of transfer of linguisitic skills acquired through analysing Evangelical-type texts to more secular subjects. In this case, they have a clear arts/language bias. The results in biology and Spanish, whilst showing no clear significant differences, nevertheless indicate that Evangelical students accounted for all the "A" grades in Spanish and over half the "A's" in Biology. This last finding is intriguing, given that there has recently been a resurgence of Creationism both in the UK and North America, and the study of Biology necessarily involves evolutionary theory. But it is an important subject for aspiring medical students and obviously the utilitarian consideration outweighs any ideological threat the subject might be thought to pose.

At A-level (17+) a somewhat different picture emerges among those who had sat the exam with no significant differences in grades between the two groups although Mainline students were on average taking a greater number of A-levels (79 per cent taking 3 A levels compared with 73 per cent of Evangelicals). This finding may be the result of a variety of personal, social and academic factors. In personal and social terms, the Mainline students at age 15-16 may be entering a phase of "finding" themselves, of coming under greater peer influence to go to discos, to try alcohol, tobacco and the other "worldly" accompaniments of modern youth culture at the expense of their academic progress and then at a later point may have settled down to some extent as the imperatives of A-levels, higher education and career choices come more clearly into view. The attitude survey would, however, suggest that the Evangelicals retain a strong sense of the divine in sustaining and deepening their personal values.

The result may also be explained by reference to the different academic demands of the two examination courses. The gap between GCSE and A-level in terms of the intellectual demands on students is substantial and the latter examination calls upon greater use of analytical, interpretive and perhaps crucially, in this case, critical skills. Evangelicals coming from a background where unquestioning diligence is highly valued could be expected to achieve good results at GCSE where there is greater emphasis than at A-level on the steady accumulation and application of factual material. It may be that the more theologically and socially liberal theological background of the Mainline students enables them more readily than Evangelicals to develop critical analyses and insights into A-level texts, articles and so on. This factor could therefore act as a levelling agent with regard to the apparent Evangelical advantage at GCSE level.

Deep-structural patterns

The analysis set out above gives a picture of the two groups' attitudes towards academic, personal and moral spheres of their lives. By its nature, the attitude scale developed from the interview data and used in the present research can give a somewhat atomised view of the Evangelical and Mainline students' values by concentrating on their responses to individual items. Further analysis through clustering by means of factor analysis can make clear any underlying patterns of attitudes among any particular sample. Cohen and Manion suggest that "Factor analysis ... is particularly appropriate where the investigator aims to impose an orderly simplification upon a number of interrelated measures". (1989, p. 365) For a full discussion of the technical details of the procedure Child D (1970) provides a concise and comprehensible account.

The combined Evangelical and Mainline survey data were initially factorised using the SPSS techniques. This resulted in the extraction of six clusters three of which were indeterminate and eliminated from a second 3 factor analysis.

Factor one: Commitment

This consisted of 7 questionnaire items set out below in order of strength of contribution to the factor (See Appendix I):

> Item 20
> Item 8
> Item 11
> Item 16
> Item 14
> Item 1
> Item 19

One of the advantages of factoring is that it allows the researchers room for interpretation of "hard" statistical data derived from attitude scales. Its disadvantage lies in the difficulty sometimes of finding a common thread within which to link the individual contributory items. There is also the problem of extrapolating too "creatively" from the factor structure. In this case all 7 items are strongly represented (all loading above 0.60) and appear to cluster around a concept of commitment. In the first item (20) this is expressed in the general context of achieving success in life as a means of glorifying God or alternatively as a more personal attainment whilst acknowledging in this the importance of family support. In the second (8) the degree of commitment to bible study is perceived as the main contributory element towards academic competence and similarly with the third item (11) where strength of religious belief is the central feature relating to the factor. The fourth component (16) is focused specifically on examination success and the extent to which assurance of belief in God or individual hard work can assist performance. In the last 3 items (14, 1, 19) the emphasis is shifted towards personal values and the extent to which their quality can be gauged by a person's religious commitment.

This grouping of items and its statistical pre-eminence together form an important reference point in the lives of the present sample of Evangelical and Mainline students; the underlying element appears to be a *commitment* to religious belief as a way of regulating moral behaviour, and in establishing personal values. This is clearly illustrated by reference to the interview data where an Evangelical student was able to draw a line between acceptable and unacceptable activities in her social life. This occurred usually when she was asked out by non-Evangelical friends and her acceptance was determined by the likelihood of discos, dancing, or other "unsuitable" activities becoming part of the evening's entertainment.

The two groups' factor scores differ significantly (p = 0.000) with regard to this grouping of items. For the Evangelical sample, a concept of self is synonymous with their religious beliefs. These form a prism of core values through which the world is interpreted and acted upon according to how that social, personal and academic involvement fits with their own religious values.

The Mainline sample tend to see commitment to moral, academic and career values as related to more secular values. They agreed more readily that "My success in exams is due to my own hard work" rather than "I feel secure in the knowledge that God will always help me through exams". Neither did they hope for success as solely a means of glorifying God relating this more directly to personal satisfaction and family approval "I want to succeed in life for myself and my family". There is a clear impression from the Mainline sample of greater separation between religious belief and academic and other social and personal values. As far as future career is considered this is clear in their view that they were unlikely to "have considered a career in line with God's will" and similarly they took the view more strongly that success in academic achievement was not influenced by belief in God (11). By contrast with Evangelical personal values they were more likely to believe that "morality and personal goodness can be achieved even without any religious belief" (14).

Taking these together the Mainline students, not unexpectedly, are less committed to religious beliefs as the underlying regulatory theme in their lives. This is not to argue that they are any less concerned with acquiring worthwhile personal, moral and social values and living their lives in line with them. They appear to have a more open-ended, liberal interpretation of the sources of academic success, personal morality and the motivation for future career choice.

Factor 2: Achievement

This was made up from a group of 5 items listed below in order of significance of contribution to the factor.

Item 2
Item 3
Item 5
Item 7
Item 10

This factor has a clear secular structure when the contributing items are taken together. In the questionnaire survey there were also five of the seven items where there were no significant differences between the Evangelical and Mainline students. The factor structure suggests an underlying theme of motivation towards academic success and it is important to note that there was no difference in factor score between the two groups of students. Interpretation of factors is always complex and in this case there appears to be a contradiction with the first grouping of items in factor one where the emphasis was related to religious commitment as a pivotal element in all aspects of living. Here both sets of students appear to be focused on achieving success at school and university against the more secular background of family support, encouragement of teachers, personal ambition and an element of intellectual curiosity. Given the high average ability of both samples this result is quite consistent with their successful experience of education. By definition of where they are (sixth form and university) they have already substantial achievement behind them. It may be that the two samples, whilst strongly motivated, approach such values from different perspectives, the Mainline from a secular viewpoint and the Evangelical group on the basis of their religious values. For the latter group there appears to be no conflict between the two sets of values; academic achievement or, personal morality and the expectation of future career success, are all subsumed in their religious beliefs originally and still described by many Evangelicals as their "calling" in the world.

Factor 3: Independence

A group of 6 items set out below contributed to this factor.

> Item 4
> Item 6
> Item 9
> Item 12
> Item 13
> Item 17

The first two contributory and most heavily weighted items appear to cluster around the idea of independence with respect to academic work and relations with others. The samples' scores on these two items show significant differences with the Mainline students emerging as the more collaborative group who were also more willing to help other students. This is supported by responses to another aspect of the factor, item 12, where there is a significantly greater idea of religious separation and independence among Evangelical students.

Conclusion

Steve Bruce in "Firm in the Faith" (1984) argues that modern Evangelicals are "comfortable with modernity" in reaching an accommodation with twentieth century capitalism. This, he argues, enables them to retain an ethic of separation in doctrinal and theological matters whilst simultaneously sanctioning material success in business and the professions. The present study would indicate that Evangelicals' accommodation to modernity, which Bruce discusses, is not as definite a moral or theological landmark as it at first sight may appear. It is arguable from the present empirical and interview data that Evangelical students retain significant elements of the original ethic of "this-worldly asceticism" which Weber argues emerged during the Reformation in the 16th and 17th centuries.

Whilst the picture emerges of both groups of students as highly motivated towards academic and future career success the Evangelical students are marked out by the extent to which for them religious belief is still a potent source of moral energy and material aspiration. They are clearly aware of this in their perception of themselves as "set ... apart from other students and their lifestyle" and in terms of career "... I feel I may choose a career in line with God's will." In these and a range of other responses to the survey data an ethic of doctrinal and moral separation remains a bedrock for the definition and acceptability of most aspects of everyday living.

"God's will" appears to have an over-riding importance for this sample of Evangelical students as a reference point in their desire for academic achievement and in their ambition for material success. This is expressed clearly in the context of "glorifying God"; that "God will always help through exams"; in wanting "to succeed in life to glorify God"; and in being "confident that I will do well because I trust that God will bless my efforts".

In terms of moral behaviour Evangelicals differ from Mainline students believing that it is only through "Christian teaching that we can be morally upright" and similarly "...my religious ideals have made me a more conscientious person in all aspects of my life". In terms of academic progress, Evangelicals also see bible reading as a core aspect of their religious practice generating cognitive benefits believing that "... Bible study has made me more competent with academic work".

These values lend support to Weber's view that post-Reformation Puritans were distinguished by the extent to which they expressed their religious beliefs in the hurly-burly of business, the professions, school, politics, social life and entertainment. Such beliefs contrasted sharply with a more cloistered approach to religious practice and in the established church's ambivalence during the middle ages towards the making of profit and the practice of usury, charging interest on capital lent. Those who practised it, the money lenders, where excoriated as moral pariahs.

In economic terms, Evangelicals whilst accepting material success and wealth in the process of practising an ethic of "this-worldly asceticism" nevertheless still wish to remain distinct from other aspects of modern secular society. This accommodation between secular and religious value systems has been, in large measure, a consequence of Wesleyan interpretations of the doctrine of predestination. These were the culmination of changes which had been introduced over time as the initial bleakness and hopelessness of the doctrine was ameliorated by Puritans in order to provide greater meaning to their lives. Methodist teaching the 18th century was influenced by Arminiu's (1560-1609) doctrine of free will in achieving salvation rather than Calvin's (1509-1564) more involuntary view that only God could know who was to be one of the elect. The majority of Methodists preached (Whitefield remained a Calvinist) that you could be saved and know it by virtue of being free in conscience to choose and practise the sort of life which led to salvation. Wesley's ideas contained a more democratic ethic by arguing that such a choice and its rewards in heaven were open equally to the factory owner and shop floor worker who provided the backbone of the industrial revolution. The present findings indicate that the beliefs of 19th century working class labourers still resonate in the values of and lifestyles of their now mostly middle class descendants, in terms of the osmotic nature of their religious doctrines and pursuit of worldly success.

In summary, there appear to be two strikingly dissimilar discourses being enacted. For Evangelicals in the present study one is distinguished by the primacy of their religious beliefs and doctrines in forming social and moral values and as the basis for their motivation towards academic and material success. It is arguable that this represents the current status of a historical process involving the reconciliation of Evangelicals' beliefs and lifestyles with the increasing secularisation of late 20th century living.

By contrast the Mainline sample's co-ordinates of belief, lifestyle and future ambitions are considerably less doctrinal, in a conservative Evangelical sense. They appear to reflect a view that belief, and morality, social activities career and so on are best interpreted according to their respective provenances; that deriving moral values from an inerrantist view of scripture, for example, may present very real dilemmas in the circumstances of practical living. In other aspects of life, the Mainline students take a more secularly existentialist approach to both choosing a career having "never really considered a career in line with God's will" and similarly in relating academic achievement to more secular individualist virtues that the Evangelical sample who were inclined towards the belief that God's help was an important contributory factor in doing well at school.

Notes

1. These terms are used in their colloquial rather than their sociological sense, i.e. of church - domination - sect - cult continuum; interviewees would describe themselves as, for example, Church of Ireland or COI.
2. There is only a 1 in 1000 probability that the result is due to chance.

4 Exemplar interviews

The analysis so far has concentrated on the relationship between belief and academic values in terms of success at school. This chapter takes the discussion further by expressing the views of a small number of people who have achieved success in their chosen careers. In their case the interviews focussed on the religious background for career choice and the extent to which it provides motivation for career advancement and material wealth..

A number of in-depth interviews was carried out with a group of "exemplar" Evangelicals. These interviewees were not in an exact sense "ideal types"; but were, rather, senior or leading figures in business or professional life who shared an Evangelical background and who were mostly still "practising". Interviews were conducted in Northern Ireland and North America. The individuals were respectively a surgeon, a university lecturer, an Emeritus professor of Classics, a diplomat, a retired headmistress, a rancher and a veterinary surgeon

Cohen and Manion (1989) list as one of the purposes of the interview "for testing or developing hypotheses, for gathering data" (p. 271) and it was felt important to discuss with leading Evangelicals and ex-Evangelicals their experiences of childhood and adolescence in the context of home, church and school. Cohen and Manion also discuss the range of interview techniques available and mention "the completely informal interview where the interviewer may have a number of key issues which she raises in conversational style instead of having a set questionnaire". (p. 271) This is also characterised as the "focused interview", of which they say:

> In the focused interview, however, the interviewer can, when expedient, play a more active role: he can introduce more explicit verbal cues to the stimulus pattern or even represent it. (Cohen and Manion,1989, p. 274)

As the interviews were prepared, the interviewers were conscious of the fact that the interviewees were mature and successful professional people, intelligent, articulate and well read. They were all likely to be theologically literate and, in different proportions, be widely read in reference to sociology, psychology and anthropology. With this in mind, the "exemplar" interview concentrated on a smaller range of domain issues than had been used with the sixth formers. It was anticipated that the interviews would become fluid and lengthy and develop into what is called in Italian a "conversazzione", a conversation with an intellectual structure and content. They were usually conducted in congenial surroundings, such as a study or parlour, and were frank, friendly and relaxed. The interviewer normally initiated proceedings by inviting the interviewee to comment on the interlocking nexus of home, school and church in childhood years with particular reference to academic achievement. This usually acted as a trigger for reflection on the part of the exemplar, punctuated by questions, comments and so forth from the interviewer. Throughout the session similar prompts were deployed to generate further comments.

The surgeon

The first of these interviews was with a surgeon and this is his "story". In answer to a follow-up question to the initial prompt as to home, school and church background, as to whether he characterised it as a "bookish" background he replied:

> Well, I was brought up on a farm and I don't see that as a bookish background. In fact I was one of five boys and four of us went to grammar school. We were definitely not from a bookish background.

This seemed a blunt reply; a Puritan farmer's son putting one in one's place. He was in fact a life-long Baptist from an area that had been heavily settled by Scottish Presbyterians at the time of the Plantation of Ulster. But it was striking that four of the boys went to the local selective grammar school, at a time before the 11+ examination. The farming background was obviously one which did not preclude academic and professional ambitions, and the farm was obviously prosperous enough for the sons to be allowed to attend a "traditional" grammar school (as it would have been) whose demands in terms of time spent in study would have been extensive. Most of the exemplar respondents in fact looked back on a perceived "plain and homespun" background and tended to deprecate the notion that it was overly bookish or musical. But the plain speaking Ulster Scot Evangelical often is proud to reflect on a plain and thrifty childhood and is quietly content to have moved on and up from such a base and even if manifestly much more prosperous than his parents or grandparents will not flaunt his wealth.

The "no-nonsense" bluntness is reminiscent of those austere Puritans of the sixteenth and seventeenth centuries, with their sobriety of life and demeanour and their avoidance of frivolity. Also of course to be borne in mind is the fact that the Puritans, the Wesleyans and the modern Evangelical share a consciousness shaped and informed by their being steeped in the Old and New Testaments and the characteristic bluntness and directness may run back to the "blunt Galilaean", as Jesus is called by the Oxford Hebraist, Geza Vermes (1983), because of his direct way of speech. In developing the theme as to books the surgeon was asked about bible study and hymns and replied:

> They were in the home but you were never made to sit down and read them. It was never structured in our house and it was really up to my brothers and myself to grapple with the bible in our own way. I was never compelled to do anything.

The emphasis here on the lack of coercion is striking. One remembers that for Evangelicals of each age, religious and spiritual values may be expressed in a way of life that seems austere, but that there is an accompanying quiet warmth and graciousness about such an outlook. Plainly the bible and bible-study had bulked large in the childhood and adolescence of the surgeon, but plainly also the Puritan virtues of individualism and personal effort were encouraged without any element of compulsion. The answer also pointed to there having been in the house a range of Evangelical books and aids to worship which seemed to perhaps contradict somewhat the earlier, blunt denial of there having been a bookish environment. Perhaps also there was a hint of the absence of secular literature as the focus of attention seemed to have been the bible and bible-study. As to the childhood study of the scriptures a bedrock text of Evangelicalism is contained in Paul's advice to Timothy in the second letter ascribed to him. (2 Timothy 3:14-16 NIV)

> But as for you, continue in what you have learned and have become convinced of, because you know those from whom you learned it, and how from infancy you have known the holy scriptures, which are able to make you wise for salvation through faith in Christ Jesus. All scripture is God-breathed and is useful for teaching, rebuking, correcting and training in righteousness, so that the man of God may be thoroughly equipped in every good work.

In response to a question about whether bible study had been systematic or not the reply was:

> at school age you don't really decide that you will master the book of Job ... I think that is a decision for later life. At that early age I saw bible-study as a chore.

This response points towards an early habituation to bible-study, later to develop into something more sustained and academic. Evangelical history of course is studded with well-known examples of great pioneers and their bible-study habits. Hudson Taylor, who has been dubbed the "apostle of China" was known never to miss his early morning tryst with God, over his bible. Charles Simeon, Fellow of Trinity College, Cambridge, vowed to throw a golden guinea into the river Cam, if ever he should fail to be at his bible and devotions by 4.00 a.m.; and is reputed to have once done so. The centrality of the scriptures in the Puritan consciousness is a fact taken for granted, and in modern times the Evangelical world supplies a wealth of bible study aids, ranging from Scripture Union notes for children of various ages to fully fledged commentaries on individual books of the Bible, as well as do-it-yourself manuals for teaching oneself Greek and Hebrew and parallel English-Hebrew and English-Greek versions of the bible, lineal descendants of Origen's "Hexapla" a six columned bible with the various languages and translations set out across the page. In the last decade also writers from the charismatic wing of Evangelicalism have been producing aids to devotion and bible study such as "Every Day with Jesus". One such writer to have become well-known is Selwyn Hughes. It is unclear to what extent this new type of study aid may have impinged into the traditional "Scripture Union" market, or in fact carved out a new territory.

The disciplined and systematic approach to Bible study in later years, whilst serving to feed devotion, and to foster the mental assimilation of the central doctrines of the faith, also sustains and underpins a disciplined and structured approach to life in general. In regard also to bible-study and devotions during what is called "The Quiet Time" Evangelicals cherish various scriptural injunctions as to the advisability of it taking place in the morning. "They that seek me early shall find me" is often quoted from Proverbs 8:10 AV or the story is recounted as to how the manna in the desert had to be collected before the sun rose high in the sky. The structured way of life therefore ideally includes early rising; practitioners of such devotions will hardly suffer from being late in reaching their place of work especially since punctuality is generally regarded as one of the "Calvinist virtues", and it has always been a signal virtue in business enterprises in the various stages of capitalism.

Asked about Sunday school attendance the interviewee replied:

> Yes, church twice on Sunday and Sunday School in the morning and young people's meeting on a Friday night.

A striking research finding from the interviews and questionnaires of the sixth form sample related to the considerable amount of time devoted to church activities per week amongst Evangelical students by comparison with the relatively short periods of time invested in church by Mainline students. The surgeon also mentioned that Saturday afternoon was devoted to private bible study. Thus, from Friday evening until late Sunday, the weekend was dominated by bible-centred and church-related activities. This programme was fitted into the ongoing life of a busy farm and attendance at a traditionally academic grammar school and clearly laid the foundation of what Weber called "this worldly asceticism". Such an outlook, he went on to argue, where the values underpinning worship, study and career are indistinguishable, resulted in a material success which was not perceived as compromising Puritans' spiritual values. Success in fact was confirmation of the worth of their values. There seems to have been little room for frivolity or "worldliness". There is a resonance here back to the Lutheran notion of "work as a calling", a sanctified "vocatio" from God. Davidson and Caddell find in a study of "Religion and the Meaning of Work" that:

> Consistent with Weber's thesis, religion provides a framework within which some people (15 per cent of our sample) come to think of work as having some sacred significance. Our findings suggest that simply being a church member and being exposed to religious influences is not enough (denominational affiliation, pastoral influences, and sermons had no effect). But when religion is internalised, it causes some people who are already inclined to think of work as important to take the additional step of viewing it as a calling, not just a career (Davidson and Caddell, 1994, p.145).

Added to the notion of intrinsic religiosity supporting a religious view of work, there is the notion of separation, shared in weak or strong form by all Evangelicals. The Pauline teaching about this is quite clear in the passage beginning at 1 Corinthians 6:14 NIV:

> Do not be yoked together with unbelievers

and culminating in verse 17:

> Therefore come out from them and be separate, says the Lord (where Paul is echoing Isaiah 52:11 NIV).

A very strong form of obedience to this injunction is evident in the case of the Hutterites of North America who are so radically separated as to eschew capitalist forms of living and to practise a communitarian way of life in their Bruderhofs. Other forms of separation are more dilute than this, ranging to a softer interpretation which enjoins separation from moral evil. A set of values which prescribes a diet of work, study and worship is a kind of implicit type of separation, which may or may not be accompanied by explicit exhortations to avoid people and situations in which the religious values might be compromised. The sociology of sectarianism also suggests that groups of committed believers may feel the need to erect collective walls against the outside world. This enhances feelings of solidarity, tightens discipline and underlines the notion of cost involved in sect membership; the more sectarians have invested in an upright religious life the less likely are they to fall into laxity. Perhaps a fitting close to this section of the discussion is afforded by the quotation of the question and answer which came next:

Interviewer:

> It is not just the time thing; we are interested in the sets of values that you may have picked up and learned in the context of the home life and church life and the extent to which they were transferable.

Interviewee:

> Well, I wouldn't have been spending my time in the pub, in which case you would have had a hangover the next day as well. I would have spent my time at a young person's meeting and I wouldn't have got drunk.

The strength of feeling towards alcohol evident in the last quotation perhaps calls for a brief discussion on Evangelical attitudes towards drinking. Luther and the early Puritans liked their beer and would probably have argued that 1 Corinthians 6:10 (NIV) which excludes "drunkards" from heaven had in view excessive and habitual drinkers, the sort whom Wesley meant when he referred to converts who were "lions turned into lambs", the drunken wife and children beaters who had been converted and had reformed. But from Wesley on one can discern a growing Evangelical hostility to alcohol which eventually culminates in the temperance movements of the second half of the nineteenth century, when British Evangelicals went "political" about the issue. From about the 1770's the industrial revolution with all its accompanying social disruptions had begun to "lift off" and by the 1840's had indeed done so. J. Christopher Soper points out that :

> social change can also affect an ideology by altering the moral obligations or norms it proposes. (Soper, 1994, p.28).

So Evangelical attitudes to alcohol and the activism of the Salvation Army and the temperance movement in general are a response to misery created by the effects of rapid and massive industrialisation. Insofar as Evangelical churches have been and are actively involved with social outcasts, with drug addicts, prostitutes, alcoholics, with those who have to "come off and stay off" whatever substance it may be, then they are perennially going to manifest a "black and white" attitude to such problems, on the behalf of their continual stream of new converts. Anecdotal evidence would suggest that recently changes in attitude have been taking place; the charismatic house church movement is known not to be against "social drinking", whilst opposed to drunkenness, and the rising interest in wines and viticulture in European and American society, added to increased tourism, may be inducing some changes in Evangelical behaviour with respect to wine-drinking. Many years ago a French lady, who described herself as a "Darbyiste", that is, a member of an "assemblée des frères", a Brethren assembly, one of those planted in France, Germany and Switzerland by the Irish scholar, J. N. Darby, said to one of the authors in relation to the matter of wine-drinking amongst Evangelicals in France - "c'est le pays du vin". Probably, however, sophisticated enjoyment of wines is confined to Evangelicals in a sporadic way and mostly to those on the fringes of the movement. In the churches at large there are to be found groups of Christians who espouse a strong pro-sobriety stance, such as, for example, the Pioneer movement within Roman Catholicism. Sometimes members of such groups will put forward the argument that the wine referred to in the New Testament was non-fermented and therefore non-inebriatory but it would seem well nigh impossible to sustain such a line of argument. The comment of the governor of the feast, at Cana, reported at John 2:10 AV:

> Every man at the beginning doth set forth good wine; and when men have well drunk, then that which is worse: but thou hast kept the good wine until now;

would only seem to make sense if fermented wine were under discussion.

The interview then moved on to the notion of vocation and the attraction that medicine seems to hold for Evangelicals. In reply to the comment:

> For some Evangelicals the choice of medicine might be related to the fact that they see a further sphere for its use in Africa and elsewhere,

the surgeon said:

> Apart from that, it is a caring profession and there are 30/40 Christians in our first year (students). In most years there are 20/40 and I think the profession does attract Evangelicals. Nursing and teaching as well.

In reply to a linked question:

> Do you think they choose a career and go through a stage and say they might like to do missionary work?

He added:

> I think it might be that they would say that they would do what God wants them to do. That may or may not be overseas, it may be at home. I never had a calling to work overseas but I have a brother who has 13 years' experience teaching in Africa.

Just as the surgeon had in a sense controverted our expectations about specific transfers and had emphasised structure and discipline as general influences, so he inclined to disagree to an extent with us as to the vocation to medicine, and ideas about missionary service abroad. He was in a sense here batting with a very straight Evangelical bat, particularly in laying stress on the caring nature of being a doctor, and also including within the purview of the adjective "caring" nursing and teaching. His statistics were of interest also in terms of the high percentage of Evangelicals in first year medicine in 1991, 30/40 (out of 170). Perhaps the thinking of the interviewers at this juncture diverged from the surgeon's. Since 1793, when William Carey set out for India, Evangelicalism has been a missionary faith; in many parts of the world where people were reluctant to listen to the Christian gospel preached by Evangelicals they were nevertheless happy to welcome their medical skills. Afghanistan, for example, has long been known as a country closed to Christian missions, with the sole exception that the surgeons and doctors of the Bible Churchmen's Missionary Society were allowed in. Other missionary groups, such as, in the fifties and sixties, the Afghan Border Crusade which evangelised in the Khyber Pass area, but had no medical personnel, had to be content with contact with Afghans in transit. So the tradition of medical vocations may be related to ideas of propagating the faith in obedience to the Great Commission of Matthew 28:19 NIV:

Therefore go, and make disciples of all nations, baptising them in the name of the Father, and of the Son, and of the Holy Spirit.

Perhaps caring may be viewed as an element in choosing a career whilst propagation of the faith is also important. The idea also emerged in discussion that medicine, nursing and doctoring, and teaching, including in higher education, are "safe" professions carrying status and salaries, should a missionary calling not eventuate. These thoughts were not so much cynical but rather an attempt to view the matter from all sides. Eventually a direct question was posed:

Are the reasons for going into medicine always money and status?

which elicited a blunt reply:

Rubbish. That's nonsense. Its never for money. It's a crazy game anyway. You would be much better doing accountancy or commerce than medicine".

This again as a response seemed to be batting with a very straight Evangelical bat. One of the factors which had engaged the attention of the researchers when the idea of the research project was first being considered and floated had been the noticeable Evangelical presence in the ranks of the consultants in the province's two largest hospitals. And as a kind of microcosm of the larger religion and career contexts interest had been stimulated by the numbers of consultants and other medical personnel attending the leading Christian Brethren congregation in Belfast, near the university campus. By way of explanation the surgeon added:

> If you are an Evangelical you do everything for the love of God and you always do your best. It is not a credit to God if you fail you exams. I should say that in medicine not many get Honours but it is nearly always the Evangelicals who get them and they collect all the medals.

This represents a cherished Evangelical conviction which is predicated on a whole range of scriptural texts. From 1 Samuel 2:30 AV:

> Them that honour me, I will honour,

through Proverbs 3:6 AV:

> In all thy ways acknowledge Him and He shall direct thy paths,

to Matthew 6:33 AV:

> Seek ye first the Kingdom of God and His righteousness and all these things shall be added unto you.

The film "Chariots of Fire" has as its major theme this idea of putting God first (by not competing in the Olympics on a Sunday) and of then being "honoured by God" (in winning a Gold Medal in another event).

In an absolute sense the point has to be conceded to the surgeon that medical consultants are not automatically going to become multi-millionaires. They invest the totality of themselves often in their service to others but in response to the query:

> Do you see investment in other things, such as your family?,

the reply was:

> Yes, indeed. There are four children altogether. Two doctors, one accountant and the youngest girl has just finished finals in physiotherapy. I really see this as an investment. They are not going to get a lot of money from me. To take a person to final MB takes about £50,000 (the cost of university training) so I think this is an investment. All my children are committed Christians and this is the greatest investment for me.

The point being reinforced here is that a surgeon working mainly for the National Health Service is not going to be excessively rich and that there is real satisfaction in having invested time, effort and money in the careers of his four children. Noticeably, too, medicine seems to have become a family tradition in this case. And there is a genuine non-materialistic ring about the notion of not leaving much money to one's offspring. Spiritually, one of the greatest aspirations of Evangelical parents is to see their children "born-again", "saved", and "following the Lord" and the surgeon is no exception; interestingly he uses the polite Evangelical circumlocution "committed Christian", which is code for "born-again", but without casting aspersions on the quality of the faith of other Christians. In a final reflective comment at the end of the interview, he said clearly that he viewed his work as a testimony:

> I don't throw the instruments around the theatre or shout at the nurses. My work should be above reproach.

He also felt that when he was operating on a patient God was guiding his hands.

The idea of testimony is a central tenet of Evangelical belief. The essential element is the idea of "witnessing to the Lord" and is deeply cherished by Evangelicals. Devout Evangelicals would feel that the duty of "witnessing" is present during every minute of the working day. Insofar as this involves a deep commitment to excellence as a surgeon it is surely one of the most attractive facets of Evangelicalism. It can be less attractive if it is interpreted to mean "buttonholing" someone on top of a double-decker bus to talk about their eternal destiny. Another attractive feature of Evangelicalism is the sense of the nearness of God possessed by believers, and the sense of dependence on Him, as expressed in the hymn:

> Leaning, Leaning, Leaning on the everlasting arms, safe and secure from all alarms. (Redemption Songs, 1891, No.377.)

Given such a proximate apprehension of the divine, it is easy to understand how the surgeon can feel that God is guiding his every movement at the operating table.

The professor

The second of the long interviews was conducted with an Emeritus Professor of Old Testament Greek, who, having retired from university life was involved in writing, translating both in modern and ancient languages and in preaching. In reflecting on his childhood he spoke of his father:

> My earliest recollection of him is in Ipswich when of an evening he would run a children's meeting for teaching and preaching. Sometimes he would have 300/400 children. It was a poor area and some would arrive with no shoes on. He could control them well but he was not so good with us kids at home. He kept their interest and he was a genius. He would get big bags of sweets for them - he had great control over them and they often cheered

when he arrived. At home he could be a different character. He taught us scriptures.

This particular "exemplar" had been born into and reared in an Evangelical home, his father being active in the propagation of the gospel to children. Since the Reformation in England it is probable that the Puritan ideology was partly passed on from parents to children; this, allied to endogamy, "marrying in the Lord" secured a familial base for the consolidation of the Puritan message. The Puritan type of Christian is also an active witnesser to the faith, so that the constituency is constantly being increased. In the case of this interviewee the early years of life had not been plain sailing:

> The family began to fall on rough times when I was four years old as this was the depression years ... my mother died when I was ten years old and my father from then found things difficult.

The impression conveyed at the initial stage of this interview was of a childhood spent in hard times of mass unemployment where the one big rock, metaphorically, was the Christian Faith. Accounts of this type abound in Evangelical literature and are frequently glossed with the notion of "the Lord providing". He may not provide luxurious abodes and sumptuous clothing but His followers believe that they will not want for the basics of survival. Evangelicals take Luke 12:22 NIV literally and seriously:

> Therefore I tell you, do not worry about your life, what you will eat, or about your body, what you will wear ... consider the ravens; they do not sow or reap, they have no storeroom or barn, yet God feeds them.

It might seem naive to have this simple faith, and to be sure, Evangelical activism has been aware of the macro-structural problems in third world poverty and has been taking appropriate action through agencies such as TEAR fund, but for many individual believers the conviction remains that the "child of God" will not want.

In answer to the question:

> At what point would you have begun structured personal bible study?,

the response was:

> I should think at about fourteen years of age. Partly because of what I saw from my older brothers and sisters in the church. It gave me a life-long awareness that there is something very special about the bible. There is a power in it and it is God's word perhaps more than any intellectual argument I know. The experience of reading the power of the bible is a crucial thing in my life. The influence was such that when at school I chose Greek and Latin instead of Physics and Chemistry. I decided to abandon the sciences.

This decision was at the advanced age of 12 years.

Structured, sequential bible study commenced for this interviewee at the age of fourteen, which probably informed his choice of the ancient languages and literatures. A perennial feature of the Evangelical academic outlook is the study of Greek, Hebrew and Latin, because the Old Testament is written in Hebrew, the New Testament in Greek, and the environment in which the New Testament stories had their setting was the Roman Empire, with Latin and Greek as its languages. It needs to be borne in mind that studying Greek and Hebrew is a more daunting task intellectually than, say, French at school or tourist Spanish at evening class. Greek is a highly inflected tongue, and involves the learning of a new alphabet. Hebrew does not belong to the Indo-European family of languages familiar to us, it exhibits alien structures, a strange and difficult alphabet, and a vocabulary with no obvious overlaps with English. Adherents of the British-Israelite theory would not concur with this last comment but the kinds of relationship they discern, as for example the Hebrew words "BERITH", covenant and "ISH"man being conflated into the adjective "British" - "God's covenant with man" are outside of the scope of linguistic theory. It is striking to remember the extent to which in Evangelical religion the study of the Bible has generated and been inextricably linked with the learning of Hebrew and Greek, and then of Latin, Aramaic Akkadian, Persian and other remote languages.

In the various "spin-off" disciplines Evangelicals have been prominent as scholars, whether it be Assyriology or Greek history. Interestingly, in view of the comments about "giving up sciences", in our excerpt, physics and astronomy have become known in recent years as disciplines which spawn Evangelical scholars who become apologists for Christianity, such as J. G. Polkinghorne, physicist and now vicar.

Ipswich as a location was in a sense a base that pointed in a certain direction:

> I got a scholarship to the local grammar school. It was expected that the brighter sparks would enter Oxford or Cambridge.

This was indeed the beginnings of the climb up the meritocratic ladder. From a background where the one parent was unemployed, the grammar school path was smoothed by scholarship money but then there lay ahead the problem of financing Oxford or Cambridge. This was partly solved by entering for a State Scholarship which involved sitting a very competitive examination and then taking the Cambridge Entrance Scholarship exam.

> I got a State Scholarship and would have liked to go to Oxford but Cambridge came first that year and it was now or never. I went to Trinity College and got a Major Scholarship - it was worth £100.

Cambridge and Oxford Colleges in the forties had 3 levels of Entrance Scholarship Award - Major and Minor Scholarships and then Exhibitions. Major scholarships were worth £100 - a veritable fortune to an impecunious student at that time, Minor scholarships were worth £60 and Exhibitions £40. The competition for these awards came from the public schools, Eton, Oundle, Rugby and so on as well as the more prestigious Grammar Schools. The difficulty of the papers was notorious; winning a Major Scholarship meant that the student was already practically postgraduate material. Once again the Bible and knowledge of it played an important part:

> On the entrance papers there was an essay. (This would have been a three hour paper). Frankly, this was my weak point. There were nine questions and I didn't even know what some of them even meant. There was one on the poetry of the Bible and this was a gift for someone with my background. I did the essay and did it well! ... I know the scriptures very well, the psalms and their academic background.

This is not so much an instance of transfer as really mastery at a high intellectual level of a particular, literary corpus, in this case the psalms. Probably at this time he would have studied and memorised them in the words of the Authorised Version, so that Tyndale's and Coverdale's cadences would have been very much in mind.[1] This was all presumably self-taught, in that the psaltery would not have been on the curriculum for aspiring sixth form Oxbridge entrants. The study of Greek and Latin poetry would in an ancillary fashion have helped a student to appreciate the art of the psalmists. But a three hour essay which helped to gain a Major Scholarship at Trinity must have been a tour de force.

As the direction of the interview swung towards music and hymnody, the question was posed as to whether they had formed an important part of the professor's life. To which the reply was:

> Yes and no. I came from a tradition with no music. Hymns were important, though, because they were theology and one would hear hymn critiques and hear older folks talking about the doctrine behind the hymns. My father was very musical but as we were poor I was put into music lessons only to be removed again.

The remark about the non-musical tradition probably refers to a Christian Brethren background. The Brethren movement split in 1848 into the exclusive and open traditions, and since then the so-called open Brethren have generally been either of a liberal or "loose" type or alternatively of a strict or "tight" frame of mind. In matters of church order Luther had taught that whatever was not forbidden in the new Testament was acceptable, whereas Calvin had argued that particular practices, such as the use of musical instruments in church, required a positive sanction, and mention in the New Testament. As musical instruments are not explicitly found there, the practice of non-musical worship became widespread, with its tuning forks and precentors. The strict party amongst Open Brethren would still adhere to this policy. It is an acute point that is made about hymns and their wording - hymns in fact are perceived as sung dogmas. Often they perform a liturgical/dramatic function, as with Christian Easter hymns, which are essentially a celebration of victory over death. Hymnody therefore is important to Evangelicals.

In the case of the Christian Brethren many of their hymns composed in the nineteenth century reveal the extent to which there prevailed amongst them a sense of eschatological awareness. The nineteenth century was one of theological ferment. On the one hand, there was the German led Higher Criticism Movement and the whole Evolution debate, on the other, groups of Evangelicals, such as the Brethren, engaged in intense speculation as to the humanity and divinity of Christ, and the question of *non posse peccare* (not capable of sin) as over against *posse non peccare* (able to avoid sinning). Sometimes an unfortunate hymn writer would get a point wrong, and then would have to recant and wear a white sheet in public.

The interview then moved on to hymns of the modern type as contained in "Mission Praise". Our interviewee was unimpressed:

> Some of the Mission Praise is direct translation from the Psalms. It is full of poor English and such repetitiveness. I find it very boring, and those terrible guitars, awful things.

At the stage of piloting research instruments we had conducted a preliminary to our "exemplar" interviews with a Baptist mathematics teacher. He had pointed out to us that in considering the possible literary transfer from hymns we were concentrating too much on a kind of classical canon of hymns, ignoring Mission Praise and in particular the compositions of Graham Kendrick. We decided to ask interviewees about this type of hymn and to inform ourselves we read through various modern hymnals and listened to tapes. We also compiled a "Graham Kendrick Corpus", to be read for comparative purposes. It is clear that much of the music and words of Mission Praise is cognate with pop music, and written at a similar intellectual level, but it has the virtues of novelty and freshness and one can see how it appeals to many people, although many others see in it a sense of repetition, invocation, of chanting a mantra, rather than of thoughtful worship.

When asked about systematic reading of missionary biography he replied:

> No, no. We would have had the occasional missionary visit to our church. My father had missionary magazines. I heard a lot about them from him.

When I went to Cambridge I knew a lot of missionaries and I would sit with them (presumably in the local church).

During this time at Cambridge the Cambridge Intercollegiate Christian Union, usually known as the CICCU, would have been very active. The CICCU had disaffiliated from the Student Christian movement in 1910 (see D. W. Bebbington, 1989) as the theological stance of the latter became more liberal and accommodating and was accordingly viewed as not being doctrinally pure. Famous alumni of the CICCU included C. T. Studd, who had sacrificed a famous cricketing future, playing for England, in the spirit of Paul in Philippians 3:7-9 NIV:

> But whatever was to my profit I now consider loss for the sake of Christ. What is more I consider everything a loss compared to the surpassing greatness of knowing Christ Jesus my Lord, for whose sake I have lost all things. I consider them rubbish, that I may gain Christ and be found in Him.

C.T. Studd and the other self-renouncing members of the "Cambridge Seven" who had all given up what promised to be brilliant careers and sporting prospects to become Evangelical missionaries had left an indelible imprint on the CICCU. Daily prayer meetings were held at lunch time in the Henry Martyn hall. Every Sunday evening an Evangelical service was held in Holy Trinity church and frequent "missionary prayer breakfasts" were held in Tyndale Hall, to encourage undergraduates to consider devoting their lives to "the foreign field" by following in the footsteps of the great C.T. and his companions. On Saturday evenings a pan-collegiate Bible study was held in a central venue such as the Debating Chamber of the Cambridge Union, led by a leading Evangelical speaker on each occasion. At five yearly intervals missions to the University were organised and led, for example, in 1952/53 by John Stott, and in 1956/57 by Billy Graham. This is the backcloth against which to situate the professor's student days in Cambridge. Nowadays he is a peripatetic speaker of world renown:

> Now I visit them in Africa and Spain, travelling widely to speak to both missionaries and their converts.

He is constantly also engaged in publishing works of Christian apologetic and exegesis which are widely read in the West and widely translated into other languages such as Russian and Romanian.

The interview then moved on to consider methods of missionary work, in particular the kind of tension that exists between the rugged, individualist pioneer and the much more organised missionary society. The professor was keen on the concept of "team":

The team is the best. As for the church, say, in Philippi controlling where Paul went, it would have been impossible anyway. They had a team and those who formed the team were responsible to the leaders of it.

The scriptural background to the discussion at this point might be summed up by contrasting two particular situations from the Corinthian correspondence of Paul. In 1 Corinthians 16:12 NIV Paul remarks vis à vis Apollos:

> I strongly urged him to go to you with the brothers. He was quite unwilling to go now, but he will go when he has the opportunity.

Those whose vision of missionary work is that a church or assembly should commend a worker "to the Lord" and dispatch them, as in the manner of Acts 13, and let the worker make his/her own decisions, would find Apollos' example here congenial. But a different situation is in view in 2 Corinthians 8:19 NIV where mention is made of the brother:

> chosen by the churches to accompany us as we carry the offering (i.e. the money collected for the poor in Jerusalem).

Here we have a plurality of churches agreeing to delegate business to an individual and some Evangelicals would find here sanction for missionary societies such as the Wycliffe Bible Translators or the Missionary Aviation Fellowship. Our interviewee adopted an intermediate position. Mention had been made of a New Testament "team" disagreeing. He replied to the point as follows (referring to Acts 15:36-41 NIV):

> I like the way Luke has recorded it in one compass of 4 paragraphs. You start off with Paul and Barnabus standing side by side, with a doctrinal dispute as on what terms people are saved, and Paul and Barnabus stick their heels in and are unbudgeable. There is a principle of salvation and so they stood together ...but Paul wasn't going to take Mark and the reason why not was because the chap absconded from earlier times when they were a team and left them in the lurch - it wasn't over basic doctrines of the faith.

He added:

> I can't see how you would run a thing like the Bible Societies or Wycliffe Translators unless you have a team or people responsible to leadership, otherwise there would be chaos. How on earth would you run a missionary hospital?

These matters might seem somewhat esoteric but one needs to bear in mind that one of the great engines that drives the Evangelical world is missionary concern, and this has been the case since the days of William Carey. Some of the missionary societies involved are vast, worldwide concerns and the monies involved are equally large, even when, as is the situation with some groups, the monies which are subscribed are unsolicited and the needs which they go to meet are unpublished. Any "neutral" sociological explanation of such situations, having, by definition, to avoid any reference to any transcendent reality might run into difficulty in explaining why people decide to contribute either publicly or privately for religious works without knowing how their money will actually be spent.

The interview ended with a discussion ranging from Weber to Tawney and back to Calvin and the question of predestination. In relation to Calvinism our interviewee clearly had Arminian leanings as evidenced by his closing remarks:

> We were brought up in love for the Lord and to serve the Lord in all we did and that would have been the motivation for doing good. When I left Cambridge I went to the North East to Durham and I was lodging among the miners. I heard about the tremendous work of Methodism over the last century and the early part of this. The miners were being converted and turned into lay preachers. They were legends by my day. They taught themselves to read because they got converted and they wanted to read the Bible. Some of them, of course, became trade unionists and politicians all over the world. Many of the chaps that learned to address the public as a preacher went on to do so as trade unionists.

This is a well-known viewpoint which would see the British Labour movement as "having owed more to Methodism than to Marx". It is a deeply rooted perception in the public mind as to the "spin-off" in secular terms from the Wesleyan ideology. As to the Calvinism/Arminianism divide the notion of "being brought up in the love for the Lord and to serve the Lord" points in a nurture rather than a nature direction, and the mention of Methodism evokes the memory of Wesley's Arminian stance. There is more of a trustful optimism about Arminianism than there is about the pessimistic determinism of Calvinism, as it is illustrated in the old Calvinist mnemonic TULIP:

T for Total Depravity;
U for Unconditional Election;
L for Limited Atonement;
I for Irresistible Grace and;
P for Perseverance of the Saints.

The diplomat

Our third exemplar interview was with a person who had been born into and brought up in an Elim Pentecostal church in a rural Ulster town. He had been deputy Editor of an Irish newspaper and was at the time of the interview a diplomat in charge of the European Union's Belfast Office. He is currently involved in broadcasting and political journalism and is the only interviewee in our "exemplar" grouping to have severed links with his Christian (and Pentecostal) past.

When asked about the nexus of home, school and church factors in his childhood he replied:

> The impact was that I was always a minority of a minority. I attended a local elementary school where you were instructed in the ways of the church. I was surrounded by Church of Ireland on the one hand and Presbyterian on the other. I was always conscious of my background especially when I won 1st prize in the Church of Ireland catechism, much to the dismay of the Church of Ireland minister concerned - a splendid man.

Here one is presented with an insight into the life of a sectarian[2] child. Expectedly, he perceived himself very much as in a minority. Protestants were in a minority in the whole of Ireland and in the forties/fifties the Elim Pentecostalists would have gained scant recognition, even from other Evangelicals. They would have been accorded the dismissive sobriquet of "holy rollers", a contemptuous reference to the ecstatic elements of Pentecostalism, of trance-like states, speaking in tongues, and of "being slain of the Lord" (i.e. going into trance and falling on the floor and rolling about). The interviewee remembered very vividly his minority sectarian background, particularly in relation to the mainline Protestant churches and their clergy. The Protestant churches of Ulster had in the early days of the state, during the twenties, transferred their schools to the then government and had been accorded, in perpetuity, the protection of the "rights of the "transferors", i.e. to be represented on the Boards of Governors of transferred and any future state schools. It was under those rights that a Church of Ireland clergyman was in the primary school, examining his charges on the Church of Ireland catechism. The cleric was not to know that the Pentecostal child who took first prize was to be a future diplomat! Historians and sociologists who have written about the Ulster problem have illuminated the grievances that stirred the nationalist population into protest at the stage of Civil Rights activism in the late sixties but very little attention has been devoted to the grievances endured by the sectarian Protestant minority, the Pentecostalists, the Brethren, the Baptists and the other scattered groups of Anabaptist-type believers. The schools transferred had, of course, been Presbyterian, Church of Ireland and Methodist bricks and mortar but the rights of the transferors were extended to "state" bricks and mortar constructed in the fifties or sixties. So graduates with a Pentecostal or Brethren background faced a bleak prospect at interview for a teaching post. It would, for example, have needed a very saintly clergyman on an interview panel to put out of his mind the fact that members of Brethren churches did not believe in clerisy. Mostly, Graduates from such backgrounds headed mostly for medicine, law or professions for which entry depended solely on academic criteria, or into business. Apart from the clerical presence on interview panels, Anabaptist-type views on "separation from the world" would have precluded the "sectarian" Evangelical joining the lodges most other folk joined - the Orange, Black and Masonic. The sociology of sectarianism of course indicates that separation may be viewed by the sectarian as obedience to scripture, but is viewed by sociologists as a requisite of sectarian discipline, or distancing mechanisms to fence off the chosen flock and keep the secular world at bay. It was perhaps to be expected that a "fundamentalist" child should have known the scriptures so well that he took the first Anglican prize! As the interview continued he was in fact asked about systematic bible study and replied:

> Systematic bible-study - no - but I was encouraged to read the bible from cover to cover. I read a bit every day but I would definitely not call that systematic - it was an obligation. One read chapters in advance.

The distinction drawn here between daily bible reading, which he felt to be a duty, and his interpretation of the adjective systematic, means that the latter term refers to something planned and structured, with appropriate accompanying aids, scholarly apparatus or notes. There must be however a literary effect in evidence if a nine year old is sequentially reading the King James Authorised Version. Anabaptist-type sectarians are usually attracted by apocalyptic genres of scripture, because of their eschatological sensitivities and have a general interest in the "End of the World" type theories or prophecies. An interesting tension arises, given on the one hand the intellectual limits of Armageddon-type scenarios and their ultimately stultifying effect on any theological discussions, and given on the other the fact that a ten year old may find the noun "heptad" in the margin of his Authorised Version. Many Evangelical sectarians use the Schofield Bible, which has marginal notes, and divides history up into seven dispensations, with emphasis on multiples of the number seven. Hence the word "heptad" appears in the marginal comments on Daniel and Revelation. Even however within a fundamentalist intellectual milieu to learn the word "heptad" it to be introduced to scholarly discourse. Systematic bible study, as disavowed by our interviewee, is also going to bring the student into contact with ancient near eastern cultures, with, as previously observed, the study of Hebrew, Aramaic and Greek, with Egyptology and Assyriology, the study of oral traditions, epic poetry and other stimulating intellectual fields. If, ultimately, such biblicism is allied with a conformist social and rural ethos an accumulation of knowledge is probable, both of a general and an esoteric type and a consolidation in some circumstances of the ideology of the sect and denomination. Where a non-conformist or revolutionary ethos obtains then biblicist devotion may produce radical effects; as Christopher Hill (1993) argues in "The English Bible and the Seventeenth Century Revolution" in the context of Puritan political radicalism.

Our interviewee did not remember any aids to bible-study:

> There were none in the house, no dictionaries or concordances. We read the bible only. My mother had a small library of devotional books which I read as a boy. Our reading was dominated by "good living books" which had been given us as school prizes. They always had a moral but never any literary style.

The absence of bible-study aids adverted to resonates with observations made by Bryan Wilson, about the Elim Pentecostal movement:

> In counselling lay preachers the leaders of the movement declare, 'We do not recommend reading a large number of books ...... you should read to remember. (Wilson, 1961, p.108).

This whole emphasis, however, reflects the social origins of those in the Elim ministry, and their distrust of formal education. It needs to be remembered of course that much has changed for Elim in the 33 years since 1961. Dr Paisley's number 2 in the Democratic Unionist Party, a Westminster MP, Peter Robinson, is an Elim adherent, as is another of the main DUP spokesmen, the schoolteacher Sammy Wilson. The "good living books" mentioned would be of the type of the "Avonlea" series, presenting edifying tales. For example, one of the main characters in "Anne of Green Gables", Mrs Rachel Lynde:

> was a notable housewife; her work was always done and well done; she 'ran' the sewing circle, helped run the Sunday School, and was the strongest prop in the Church Aid Society and Foreign Missions Auxiliary. (L. M. Montgomery, 1994, p.7.)

Such literature, of the "Little House on the Prairie" type, or the "Little Red Schoolhouse" presents moral exemplars and examples in abundance and is characterised implicitly or explicitly by a "Wilderness Wandering/Promised Land" underpinning ideology.

Clearly, this particular home background had been permeated by wholesome influences, whether directly spiritual or more temporal. In general Evangelicals down the centuries have tried to provide a healthy family and home background, stable and secure. For the first generation of converts the wholesomeness may relate to very basic matters, such as stopping drinking, as a first step in sanctification. In missionary settings a next step has often been the concreting of a mud floor and the installation of electricity in a simple way. The diplomat was second generation Elim Pentecostal and for him the social mobility meant moving from a frugal lower middle class rural market town to the Brussels bureaucracy. In a sense this represents a classic one-generation shift, as made famous by R. Niebuhr. Being a second generation Evangelical means of course that one is born into a caring and structured environment, the Puritan "virtues" of frugality and thrift are accompanied by warm and supportive intra-familial relationships. Being an adherent of an Elim Pentecostal church carried with it as a counterpoise to the Puritan start in life a certain social stigma. As late as 1965 the SCM press published a book entitled "Christian Deviations", a non-sociological descriptive lay handbook about groups such as Jehovah's Witnesses and Mormons but which also included a chapter on Pentecostals. The book as a whole was written in a generous spirit but it exemplified the sorts of social attitudes which obtained in the mainline churches towards Pentecostalism; not for nothing had there been the old adage "If you want to find the local Pentecostal church, look for the gasworks or cemetery road".

In the early sixties the Charismatic movement had just begun and there had not yet developed the kind of sophisticated apologetic later typified by the writing of theorists such as Michael Harper, the Anglican cleric who had "gone Pentecostal", and who wrote "As At The Beginning" (Hodder & Stoughton, 1965).

When the interview turned to values such as industry and diligence the response was:

> I think my background gave me a highly developed sense of duty - I don't mean an inflated sense. You did all the jobs you had to do to the best of your ability. I am very lazy and I know that I've always had to fight against indolence and I think that stems from my background. I always put my best effort into everything.

The vocabulary chosen to frame this reply is revealing. The phrase "highly developed sense of duty "seems to indicate a steadily increasing sense of moral rectitude, buttressed by a biblicist and ecclesiastical ideology. Elim churches would have been and are characterised by a disciplined regularity which typically involved "Breaking of Bread" on Sunday morning, Sunday School during Sunday afternoon and the gospel meeting on Sunday evening, a mid-week Bible-study and a mid-week prayer-meeting. This basic framework would be fleshed out by other activities such as Friday evening/Saturday morning sport for young people, frequent "salvation and healing" missions to the extent that every evening would be occupied. Open-air meetings are a feature of summer, as is tract distribution, and there would have been "tarrying meetings" during which believers would seek for "the baptism of the Holy Spirit". The phrase,"to the best of your ability" reinforces the sense of moral seriousness and dutiful application.

Weber regarded the doctrine of predestination in its strong Calvinistic and determinist sense as a kind of moral engine driving the this-worldly asceticism of the Calvinist believer in the context of a "salvation panic". The Elim teaching as to election tries to mediate on this issue. Bryan Wilson sums it up as follows:

> The eschatological teachings of the Elim movement blend with its fierce evangelism; its doctrine of the elect is accommodated with the revivalist activity of the movement. The elect is no exclusive élite already chosen, but a company into which all are invited, even though, when all invitations are answered, it will remain an elect. The movement can thus see itself as an instrument of God, extending to all a chance of salvation, even though God already knows who will accept this offer. (Wilson, 1961, p. 27.)

Trying to hold together determinism and freewill as a mystery of faith and avoiding schism by not allowing it to occupy any dominant ideological position would be characteristic of modern Evangelicalism generally, and probably has its roots in the teaching of Charles Simeon, the eighteenth century Cambridge Evangelical don who claimed to be a Calvinist at prayer and an Arminian when preaching. And one needs to remember that even where the logic of predestination is not allowed to be fully carried through, bodies such as Elim would still adhere to a traditional "hell-fire" theological position, thereby retaining an element of genuine terror. The idea of hard moral effort generated by a particular environment is again reinforced by the vocabulary of the phrase "to fight against indolence". Apart from "salvation panic" afflicting people in a general sense, as a spin-off of a particular salvation schema, there are very plain scriptural injunctions about work. When some of his converts at Thessalonica would not work in view of the imminence of the Second Coming, Paul's brusque comment in 2 Thessalonians 3:10 NIV is:

> if a man will not work, he shall not eat.

When asked about late teens and early twenties, the question posed being

> Would you have said between the years seventeen and twenty-three that 'I'm doing this task as unto the Lord',

he replied:

> I'd have said that perhaps at 17, but not at 23. At the early age of 15/16 years I began to question a lot of the formulae phrases, the clichés. I would never have said that in the company of others. I look back on my teens and twenties and I squirm. I remember taking a holiday job in St. Ives in my first year at Queen's and I refused to work on a Sunday. My employer was so astonished that he gave me Sunday off. Something was driving me then as that was a hard thing to do.

There is venerable tradition amongst ex-Evangelicals of looking back in retrospection and locating incipient doubts as to their belief-system at an age earlier than their external practice of religion stopped. Max Wright, a philosopher, has recently published a book about his upbringing and his adolescent years amongst the Brethren, entitled "Told in Gath". (This title derives from David's lament over Saul and Jonathan: (2 Samuel 1:19,20 AV)

> The beauty of Israel is slain upon the high places: how are the mighty fallen! Tell it not in Gath, publish it not in the streets of Ashkelon, lest the daughters of the Philistines rejoice, lest the daughters of the uncircumcised triumph.

In the book he draws on "Father and Son", the story of Philip and Edmund Gosse, famous Victorian father and son. The book also includes a foreword by the writer Patricia Beer on the theme of a childhood amongst Brethren and a later withdrawal from the movement. There is nothing of course particularly surprising about adolescent doubts or keeping up external sabbatarian practice. One of the problems with quantificatory approaches to secularisation theory, such as measuring religiosity by church attendance statistics, say from the GB 1851 census, is that external practice may reflect conformist and utilitarian motivation rather than conviction. Protestant Ulster is particularly sabbatarian, even in the secularised nineties. Recently the County Down Gaelic Football team won the all-Ireland Sam Maguire Cup. The North Down Council refused to congratulate them. Behind such a decision there lies a 2-nations mentality, an element of which would be the sabbatarian consideration, although the Gaelic Athletic Association's ban on members of the police and security services playing Gaelic sports is often used as justification for ignoring or snubbing Gaelic sportsmens' achievements. Traditional Evangelical Protestant perceptions of Roman Catholic religiosity would lie along the line that Catholics got mass over quickly in the morning so that the rest of Sunday was free for sport, gambling and drinking. This resonates back to the English Puritans and their attitudes to Sunday games. Evangelicals would find it difficult to accept Gaelic football finals at Croke Park as a Christian expression of joy on the afternoon of the day in the morning of which the Eucharist had been celebrated.

Comments on the interaction between the Evangelical background and intellectual life at University were revealing:

> The background made you want to give complete answers all the time. I did History and one tended to produce an essay which answered the question. ... I know now that there aren't answers for everything. I think the Evangelical background was therefore quite limiting in that sense as it didn't allow your mind to explore things. It maybe helped with some philosophical concepts. The concept of "Freedom" was very similar to the Evangelical commitment to the Lord.

This is an illuminating reply in that it suggests a kind of pilgrimage in reverse, or a transposed Damascus road experience, although it is clear from the interview that the process described is not instantaneous. A gradual slippage and drift occurs from an outlook which offers a secure, black and white religious framework for behaviour towards a different intellectual position in which it is admitted that some questions perhaps have to be left unanswered, that there is a theological and moral greyness instead of simply black and white.

One answer to the problem as to why different kinds of fundamentalism seem to command success in to-day's world may lie in the fact there is a very general hunger for and quest after meaning. People shop around in the world's ideological supermarket for a secure worldview, some of which seem to market better than others. Our interviewee is here describing a shift away from a very comforting worldview, which consists of unshakeable beliefs as the basis of ultimate meaning towards one which is rather more uncertain. The theologian James Barr feels very strongly that conservative Evangelicalism is a species of fundamentalist mental prison and has consequently written a book entitled "Escape From Fundamentalism" (1984). Barr is reluctant to concede that one can distance the concept "evangelicalism" or "neo-evangelicalism" from the concept "fundamentalism". Perhaps the metaphor of prison escape is more appropriate for a second generation sectarian than for someone who has been converted to a particular world view.

As Steve Bruce (1984) points out in "Firm in the Faith" the reason why people are converted at Evangelical revivalist rallies is that they want to be. Those endowed with the zeal of the convert are not so ready to disavow freely chosen religious beliefs. A further comment from the interviewee was illuminating in this respect:

> I was a member of the Bible Union at Queen's but I resigned because I couldn't accept the basis of their membership - they wished for a declaration to the inspired word of God. I remained friendly with them.

D.W. Bebbington comments about Bible Union groups in universities:

> Probably the most important single factor behind the advance of conservative evangelicalism in the post-war period was the Intervarsity Fellowship (IVF). (Bebbington, 1992, p. 259.)

The latter organisation had emerged during the 1920's and had been formally established in 1928 as a body for those university students who followed the Cambridge Inter-Collegiate Christian Union when it separated from the Student Christian movement. Its basis of faith was resolutely conservative but by no means extreme. The first clause for example affirmed not the inerrancy of the Bible but the "infallibility of scripture, as originally given". Bebbington draws a nice distinction here between "inerrancy" and "infallibility". What the writers of the basis of faith probably meant was that the original manuscripts of scripture, now lost, were infallible in matters of faith and morals. What prompted the interviewee's resignation was probably the fact that in a Belfast university in the fifties the de facto interpretation accorded to the wording was that it connoted inerrancy, including matters of biology, geology and history.

It is a truism of course in the sociological study of religion that conservative groupings who refuse to accommodate liberal insights into statements of faith tend to remain stronger bodies, in terms of attendance, subscriptions and so on than those who accept more diffuse credos. Steve Bruce (1984) charts the long decline of the SCM as its views became more and more radical. The diplomat's comments about "remaining friendly" with former Evangelical Bible Union colleagues are echoed frequently in the literature of those who write about an Evangelical past with which they have parted company. Frequently a sense of nostalgia is apparent, a feeling of regret at having left a club, a network of warm and attractive friends. Some, such as the Max Wrights, the Edmund Gosse's, the Patricia Beers eventually write in such a manner as to render the break irremediable, others try to maintain bridges of friendship in the spirit of Dr. Barnardo, who in referring to a period of time spent amongst Brethren said that: "it was a good street to have passed through".

After university, in later years, the tension between conservative ideological positions and liberal ones still troubled the interviewee:

> I then went to work in Addis Ababa for the Lutheran World Federation. The job had been advertised in the Times and they were looking for a Christian journalist to set up a radio service. The language was still upsetting me and I needed to find a language which was relevant to to-day's world. (by "language" is meant Evangelical discourse)

An autobiographical picture emerges here of a stage in personal development at which a conservative interpretation of Christianity is receding but the "pull" of Christianity, as liberally interpreted, is strong enough to lead to choosing Christian radio journalism as a career option. James Barr (1984) speaks pessimistically of fundamentalism as a kind of prison but Horton Davies (1965) referred to the tendency of second and third generation sectarians to move into the mainline churches and to the invigorating effect such arrivals often had on their ecclesiastical hosts. Pentecostal grandchildren deciding to move into the local Presbyterian church bring with them a culture of activism and generosity. They tend to throw themselves into all aspects of church life and have frequently been used to donating a tenth of their income to Christian causes.

The drift continued. In reply to the question:

Would you still have any Evangelical or Christian vocation? Grapple with the book of Job?,

the reply was:

It has all faded. After Ethiopia I tried to find a church and eventually found a Methodist Church in Dublin. ... It had many Catholic mixed marriages, Church of Ireland etc. ... I was elected as a congregational representative. In the end I resigned because I was faced with either being disruptive or saying nothing.

This is an example of what must very often happen. A former fundamentalist, unable to accept that particular interpretation of Christianity, shops around for another ecclesiastical berth. There are the children to think about; but he also happens to be an active, dynamic, literate professional person. If he is thrust into a position of prominence in a congregation he may encounter difficulties, perhaps because he sees that the minister lacks administrative competence. Or he may be theologically more widely read than the minister or senior elders. Very often such talent is successfully integrated into the ongoing work of a parish. Peter Berger (1969) adverts to the way in which in the U.S.A the process of bureaucratisation in churches is spurred on by the fact that the churches draw on the professional and business expertise of their flocks. For the present exemplar the final parting was at base an intellectual one:

The young minister from Cork was painfully aware that he did not have the answers to the world's problems but he was replaced by a Minister from N. Ireland who thought that he had all the answers. I found him exquisitely boring. ... When I came back to Belfast I never felt a need to go back to any church.

It is tempting to speculate that here we have a picture of someone who at an emotional level could never really settle down in a big, liberal church, having been brought up in the warmth of a sectarian "conventicle" (as Calvin dismissively described Anabaptist meetings). The intellectual issue remains complex. At one level of biblical interpretation the educated sectarian is driven to leave the sect by an issue as simple perhaps as women having to wear hats, or is simply not prepared to argue any more about how literally or metaphorically to interpret the account of Adam and Eve and the tree and the serpent. But the grass is not always green on the other side of the fence. The large, "liberal" church, may have its own dogmatic inflexibilities. Perhaps a "high" doctrine of the sacraments obtains and there is pressure for children to be baptised and confirmed, and social censure ensues if this does not happen. Or it may be the case that part of the sect's teaching is actually a correct interpretation of scripture. Bryan Wilson (1990) makes the point that the Exclusive Brethren are excoriated for refusing to eat with non-observant fellow-believers but that in fact they are simply following Paul's instructions in this matter (1 Corinthians 5:11 NIV).

> But now I am writing to say you must not associate with anyone who calls himself a brother but is sexually immoral or greedy, an idolator or a slanderer, a drunkard or a swindler. With such a man do not even eat.

Or the ex-Elimite may conclude that if scripture is infallible and does not contradict itself then the Pentecostal arguments as to speaking in tongues (glossolalia) are unanswerable.

The lecturer

Our fourth exemplar interview was with the daughter of a Baptist pastor who had grown up and been educated in Ulster. She had graduated in modern languages and had taught for a time in a large Belfast voluntary grammar school. She had added to her primary qualifications and at the time of the interview was a university lecturer in accountancy.

The interview began with the invitation to reflect on her religious upbringing. Commenting on the time spent in church activities she said:

> I was teaching 7 year olds in Sunday School and I would spend 2-3 hours on a Saturday night preparing overheads and things. I attended Bible study classes for 2 hours per night and then I joined an older Teens and Twenties Study group - (1 hour per week).

This was an interesting reply in that Saturday night was singled out for mention. Interviews with the sixth formers had revealed quite striking numbers of hours invested in church activities. Contemporary scholarly discussion invokes a vocabulary drawn from economics in describing religious commitment to a church or denomination or sect and the cost to the individual. If, outside of work, all one's spare time is invested in church-related activities then one can use the terms "high-investment and high cost". The "price" will usually be balanced by rewards in terms of social and emotional benefits. The hours spent in Bible study and Sunday school teaching will be rewarded in terms of the positive emotions generated within the social group, as part of a local Baptist congregation and in the context of the larger Baptist community. Of course, worldwide, as opposed to minority status in Ulster, Baptists constitute the largest Protestant denomination.

A general impression has been created by the research to the effect that second and third generation adherents of Evangelical churches experience an extensive socialisation into the serious, disciplined and "wholesome" worldview of the church. Because it is strong and positive the children and adolescents involved do not have to be inducted into a separatist ideology with negativistic overtones. Any sense in which they "miss" the disco, or feel "out of it" in school because they do not attend pop concerts is mitigated by the extent to which Evangelical churches fill the social vacuum for them.

In answer to the question about aids to Bible study the reply was predictable.

> There were lots of books in the house. Occasionally I consulted commentaries and concordances. However, I usually used Scripture Union notes.

There is a modesty evident here, as evidenced by the claim mainly to have used Scripture Union notes. The Scripture Unions were founded in 1897 as an offshoot of the Children's Special Service Mission founded itself in 1867 to evangelise at seaside resorts amongst children. As a world-wide organisation the Scripture Union supplies daily Bible-reading notes of an undenominational nature for children of all ages. It thus provides, within a conservative Evangelical interpretation, a systematic study guide to the Bible. Recent Scripture Union publications such as Dr. F. Bridger's "Children Finding Faith" (S.U 1988) illustrate that the construction of Bible-study notes is now supplemented by insights drawn from the work of developmentalists such as Piaget and Kohlberg. In the case of this exemplar Bible study of a systematic nature led to tangential Biblical topics being undertaken:

> At school three friends and myself did a New Testament Greek course ... while we were studying for our "A" levels. We never got very far. I did the course not only because of my Evangelical background but also because I am very interested in all languages.

The interviewee has a joint honours degree in French and Spanish as well as German at "O" level, and elementary University Portuguese:

> I have a need to acquire languages.

This is a further example of the linguistic interests of Evangelicals. The present exemplar is what would be termed "a natural linguist" and her Evangelical background pushes her to learn Greek. Is the interest in languages there because Evangelicals have traditionally placed the ministry of the Word above the sacraments? Or is it that their love of the scriptures "as originally given" inevitably involves the detailed study of Greek, Hebrew and Aramaic? Those with a specifically theological interest will want to read some technical German, a need which the IVF has recognised by publishing a handbook of theological German. (1971) There is also the missionary tradition in the drive to make scripture accessible to everyone by translating it into as many languages as possible. Children growing up in Evangelical homes and attending Evangelical services hear early about Hudson Taylor teaching himself so many Chinese ideograms each day as he worked behind the counter. They learn about the work of the Wycliffe Bible Translators tirelessly pushing into new areas to record and describe a tribal language, create an alphabet, teach literacy and then begin translating portions of the Bible into the new language. There appears to be some degree of a sensitising to linguistic matters. Pentecostal and neo-Pentecostal charismatic groups also take an interest in linguistic matters because of the experience of "speaking in tongues" or "glossolalia".

There is a vigorous debate as to what exactly is the relationship between the phenomena as recorded in the New Testament and speaking in tongues in the 20th century. Within the New Testament literary corpus it is also unclear whether the phenomena portrayed as happening on the Day of Pentecost can be equated with those of the "charismatic" chapters of 1 Corinthians (12,13,14) Literary criticism has also to be accommodated - perhaps Luke in chapter two of Acts is more concerned with a poetic picture of Babel reversed than with linguistic detail. Pentecostal and charismatic Christians would also not be unaware of the negative results of psycholinguistic and anthropological research into glossolalic utterance as exemplified, for example, in the work of W. J. Samarin (1972) and I. M. Lewis (1971). However, this whole dimension of what has been dubbed "The Third Force in Christendom" is an added factor in stimulating interest in linguistics and psycholinguistics.

In general academic terms, many of those Evangelicals who proceed to missionary and translation work would be in a position to draw on their fieldwork for scholarly purposes. To describe and write the grammar for a newly encountered Amerindian or Austronesian language would constitute a major piece of academic work.

In response to the question:

> You went on to become a linguist, did Bible-study and structure in the home push you forward?

The familiar lineaments of the Puritan gravitas emerged:

> I am really a workaholic by nature and I always needed to study all day and never take a break. Even now I prefer to work all day and then relax in the evening. I worked very hard at university and often worried that I should do more ... My mother insisted that all homework was done immediately after school.

A clear picture emerges of a serious home, a committed child, and concerned parents. As with the surgeon, there is no room for frivolous pursuits. The co-ordinates of existence are school and schoolwork, church and worship. Noticeably again, everyday practical living is the site of these spiritual imperatives and their secular spin-offs. If you feel that constitutionally you are a workaholic then work becomes its own reward. J. K. Hadden in a review of Stark and Bainbridge's "A Theory of Religion", comments about monastic life:

> Another reward was supplied intrinsically in the core monastic activity, intense meditation or prayer; this may be regarded not as a mode of escape, but as a form of pleasure seeking, a technology for producing what the Buddhists call bliss (Hadden, 1993, p.403).

The monks practised an other worldly asceticism to achieve "bliss" - in the this-worldly asceticism of the Puritan believer there is evident an element of "bliss" in sustained hard work.

As was to be expected from a child of the manse she grew up well acquainted with missionaries, missionary biography and literature:

> Up until I was eleven years old we had a lot of visiting missionaries and they always came to Sunday dinner. I knew them personally and the books were also in the house for me to read. Mostly Carey, Hudson Taylor etc.

Evangelical Christian missionaries are sometimes viewed as somewhat outmoded remnants of the Victorian era. A Marxist perspective on Victorian missionary activities would of course have been that the ideology came after the bayonets, the ideology being that of a burgeoning, exploitative and colonialist capitalism. Some Victorian missionaries undoubtedly conformed to the stereotypical Aunt Sally, but the annals of the more quietist and pietistic Evangelical missions are filled with tales of heroism and self-sacrifice. A medical missionary nowadays perhaps is often seen in this light within the Evangelical world precisely because medical missions were the cutting edge of Evangelical outreach. Also, because so many of the Evangelical missionaries believed in the priesthood of all believers, or the autonomy of the local church, or in similarly "low" doctrines, they tended to adopt native dress, to train locals for eldership and for medical work. They avoided the paternalism which so often characterised liberals such as Albert Schweitzer, who, although he built a hospital at Lambarene in the Congo never trained a single African doctor or dentist. Frequently, Evangelical missions have been or are accused of destroying the balance of a native culture and of reducing converts to camp-followers of American consumerism. The Sunday Times has from time to time attacked the New Tribes Mission on these grounds, or indeed that in countries such as Paraguay or Bolivia they have co-operated with right wing regimes in civilising the Indian jungle and montagnard populations.

The Daily Telegraph (8 November 1994) reports that the Pacific Conference of Churches is seriously concerned that 20% of islanders in the South Pacific now belong to New Religious Groups. These groups are fundamentalist and whilst not subscribing to blatant racism, advocate white values and white images - their publications present as models: "healthy, clean, and well dressed white people"; the converts tend to be politically passive and do not participate in strikes, demonstrations or blockades to make demands of governments or employers". Such inactivity apparently is welcomed by governments committed to free-market economics. Thus the missionaries stand accused of "gentling" the masses.

The anthropological literature makes no value judgements as to the ontological status of shamanistic practice as over against that of orthodox trinitarianism, but, particularly in the case of South America, Evangelical Brazilians, Colombians and Venezuelans tend to say:

What do you want us to do with the Indians, leave them naked in the jungle?

Our interviewee puts William Carey at the head of list, as one would expect from a Baptist. Asked if she had herself thought of a missionary vocation she gave a typical reply:

No. I don't think that it is something that you would have chosen to do. God would have chosen it for you and you would have done it. You really did not have to think about it.

This response highlights the sense of the Lordship of Christ in the life of the believer which so characterises Evangelicals. It typifies the response received from all our interviewees. If called to a missionary vocation they would all have gladly gone. A very popular hymn for Evangelical groups is:

For my sake and the gospels, go,
And tell redemption's story,
His heralds answer be it so,
And Thine Lord all the glory,
They preach His birth, His life, His cross,
The love of His atonement,
For whom They count the world but loss,
His Easter, His enthronement.

The fresh impetus which came into the Puritan spirit with the preaching of John Wesley filled people with a vision of the millions to be evangelised in England, Ireland, Scotland, Wales and the New World. This impetus shortly developed into a burning concern for the unevangelised world population as a whole. This evangelistic concern has grown and developed steadily since the days of William Carey's departure to India and now characterises Evangelical religion with but a few exceptions. In this connection modern study of the development of sects seems to indicate that a sect moves either towards isolation or in the direction of the mainstream churches. If it be an isolating sect it tends to tighten up the rules of sect discipline and membership requirements and to become introverted and unconcerned with world mission. Some Evangelical sects have done this and do not share the usual interest in world mission. The Exclusive Brethren and Hutterites would be two such.

In response to a question about older and more recent hymns and possible literary transfer she said:

> Yes, you do need to disentangle hymns. The other thing now is ...... children now don't understand how English is formed, they have lost grammar, structure and analytic processes. English was one of my best subjects and even in Primary 7 I was enjoying Dickens. I had a very good vocabulary and I think that was because my mother always insisted that we used a dictionary for any new words. I read a lot and understood any word in context, my leisure reading would still be Dickens, Jane Austen and French and Spanish novels.

The question about hymnody generated an answer that broadened out to incorporate observations about reading in general. There is also a nostalgia for traditional teaching of English - instruction in the parts of speech and clause, kind and function analysis are obviously viewed as important features of English teaching which have been abandoned. It would be illuminating to ask a substantial number of Evangelicals what were their views on "modern" approaches to the pedagogies of English and history, with their emphasis on the thematic and the experiential. It is tempting to speculate that the emphasis on the inspired Word and on the exact meaning of Biblical terms would influence Evangelicals towards a traditional and conservative approach, and hence to favour traditional approaches to grammar, and in history a chronological rather than an empathic pedagogy. It would be interesting also to elicit Evangelical attitudes towards the controversial notion of a literary canon; there has been a struggle recently between Education Ministers, who insist on a canon and the Association of English Teachers which views such a concept as restrictive and limiting. Pushing matters further it seems hardly likely that Evangelicals would favour modern deconstructionist approaches to literature.

The home background is again shown in this reply to have been structured and supportive. The discipline of constant use of a dictionary is likely to increase vocabulary at an exponential rate, and no doubt transfers to reading in foreign languages. By contrast with some of the other busy professional exemplars such as the surgeon and the vet the lecturer reads for leisure trilingually.

Asked about a sense of vocation and choice of subjects she replied:

> Basically I took the subjects because I liked them. I never knew what I wanted to do as a career. My first choice was to take a literary degree but I didn't like pulling it apart and much preferred the language - Philosophy/ French/Spanish ..... I took psychological and aptitude tests and the profile revealed that I should have been a scientist.

Perhaps being the daughter of a pastor makes one rather more practical and pragmatic. The interviewee chose to pursue her favourite subjects and seems not to have gone through any period of agonising over God's will, as was the case with some of the sixth formers/undergraduates. The Keswick Convention tradition within Evangelicalism, rather like the Buchmanite Oxford movement, has a record of encouraging spiritual introspection. This can lean in the direction of a kind of Evangelical mysticism and the kinds of biographies or apologias recommended would be those of Borden at Yale, who wished to undertake a missionary vocation in one of the most difficult parts of the world and therefore espoused celibacy, or the story of John and Betty Stam, who had fallen in love in the USA in the thirties, but in response to separate missionary vocations had parted and gone their separate ways to meet up later in China and marry and eventually to be executed by the Communists as capitalist spies, or of Isobel Kuhn, of China, who agonised at having to send her young daughter to boarding school. The lecturer seems to have made her choices in a very down to earth and almost purely secular manner.

As to her having been accorded a profile suggesting a scientific career Steve Bruce (1984) argues that the cognitive style of conservative Protestants is essentially similar to that of exponents of old style Baconian natural science. He comments that in the light of such a conclusion it is not surprising to find that so many scientists and medics are to be found amongst British Evangelicals. Perhaps it also chimes in with this scientific penchant that the interviewee left teaching for lecturing in accountancy. Perhaps, if one has the choice of subjects, accountancy is a particularly congenial area for an Evangelical. The Puritan divines of the sixteenth century used to keep "account books" with God; a practice based on the Johannine text 1 John 1:9 AV:

> If we confess our sins, he is faithful and just to forgive us our sins, and to cleanse us from all unrighteousness.

It was a frequent Puritan exhortation "to keep short accounts with God", i.e. to make a regular practice of reviewing, confessing, and having one's sins forgiven (in the solitude of one's devotions of course - there being "one Mediator between God and men -the Man Christ Jesus" (1 Timothy 2:5 AV)).

Perhaps the keeping of such spiritual diaries was influenced by the general Calvinist emphasis on good book-keeping as a part of modern business practice. So there was for the interviewee a very uncomplicated and pragmatic beginning to professional life.

The interview was rounded off with a generalised discusion of the Weber thesis in relation to Ulster Evangelicals. Amongst her concluding comments were:

I don't know. A colleague of mine who is Church of Ireland says it is the Baptists and the Brethren who do well. It is something that I have noticed about the Brethren - they always seem to do well. Part of it could be the idea that whatever you do you should do well - even if that means making money. From a cynical point of view it could be like "Chariots of Fire" - the hero has the idea that if you honour God you will prosper. Coming back to the idea of being honoured by money. Another element is perhaps that the assemblies seem to look after their own.

(Christian Brethren churches are frequently designated "the assemblies" - a usage which has grown up because Brethren eschew traditional nomenclatures - but "assembly" is simply a different English rendering of the Greek ···ekklhs¢ia - ekklesia.)

Weber in his survey of entrepreneurial practice was concerned to single out quite numerically small specific groups such as Mennonites and Quakers and it is illuminating here to find a Baptist singling out Christian Brethren as particularly prosperous. BBC Ulster had some time before this interview conducted a "spoof" car programme on the latest models in the car park at a large Christian Brethren assembly. Ill-feeling had ensued as the producer and his automobile experts had not asked the permission of the elders of the meeting concerned. The Christian Brethren would be regarded as a solid constituency within the larger corpus of Evangelicals in Ulster. Numerically such groupings tend to be insignificant in comparison with the mainline churches. According to the 1981 Northern Ireland census 339,818 people regard themselves as Presbyterians. People who overtly claim to be Brethren number in contrast 12,158, although probably a goodly proportion of those who called themselves solely Protestant (14,318) or Christian (8,695) would in fact be Brethren. Autonomous local churches, because they are in fact independent entities, do not have any central headquarters to which to submit statistics, hence accurate figures are difficult to obtain. Impact on the community is probably in inverse proportion to numbers because members of voluntaristic groups such as the Brethren or Elim (3,413) are individually committed and are not nominal; each adherent would, in the words of 1 Peter 3:15 AV be:

ready always to give an answer to every man that asketh you a reason of the hope that is in you with meekness and fear.

The comment about "the assemblies looking after their own" is again a kind of intra-Anabaptist family remark, a comment on the perceived fact that members of such groups as Christian Brethren care for each other in practical as well as spiritual concerns.

The North American exemplars

The transatlantic "exemplar" data is drawn from a number of interviews conducted in the area of South Saskatchewan/North Dakota and South British Columbia/Washington state. The first interviewee was a prosperous rancher whose land lay along the 49th parallel. He was an adherent of an evangelical church of the area. The same interview framework was used as had been with the Ulster exemplars.

The rancher

Invited to reflect on the interlocking nexus of home, church and school, he said:

> As a child I would say I was fairly strictly supervised and brought up and then when I got away from home to school I suppose I headed for the extreme opposite and I think that I'm correct in thinking that because I can remember my brother trying to correct me when I was away from my parents.

Here again there emerges the picture of a strongly structured and controlled home background during childhood and adolescence, evocative of Puritan manuals of childrearing. Bebbington (1989) argues that Evangelicalism as we know it arose particularly with Wesley; this study has indicated the powerful influence which Wesley exerted on the development of Evangelicalism but against Bebbington we would discern the roots of the movement as firmly rooted in the sixteenth century Puritans and beyond. The exemplar interviews, in succession, point to childhoods passed in a world where the twin axes of worship and work bulk large against an austere yet warm background of structured family life. Max Wright and Patricia Beer, in the tradition of "Father and Son" savagely caricature such pietistic childrearing practices in terms of the negativities they attribute to them but such bitterness did not characterise any of our exemplar reflections. Children and adolescents brought up in such structured domestic and ecclesiastical backgrounds are frequently regarded as having been indoctrinated but our interlocutor here was keen to avoid any such suggestion. In answer to a question about whether bible-study had been systematic or not he replied:

> Not at that stage of my life. It included systematic bible reading, but not where we were, can I use the word - forced -, not forced in any way, to study and come up with answers, we were at that time of life, and when I say we, there was only my brother and I in my family at that time, two sisters later on, I think that we were just exposed to bible reading without one and, I think I can honestly say, unbiased comment to it, but we were not taught anything that was not quite obvious.

The practice of reading the bible "round the table" with each member of the family reading a portion, and with parental comment, exhortation and prayer, referred to in North America as the "family altar" is clearly in view here. Generally speaking, the data suggest that secularising influences have eroded this practice in Ulster, but that it still features in United States and Canadian Christian practice. It is a commonplace in the debate about secularisation to point out that North American patterns of religiosity include a higher "civic" element than do British or European. Higher church attendance in the USA perhaps is predicated on the fact that American churches perform a wider role in regard to community affairs, particularly where churches are carriers of ethnic culture and identity. The film "The Deerhunter" opens with a scene in which a very "American" suburb celebrates a very "Orthodox" (Ukrainian) wedding. Other images and practices which re-inforce or celebrate notions such as "the little house on the prairie" may evince a tenacity not observed in Europe because of underlying cultural imperatives. Indeed, a standard European comment on the Niebuhr argument about the classic shift along the sect/denomination/church continuum is that Niebuhr had in view the "melting pot" of the USA, with rapid demographic change, swift patterns of social mobility, the "Americanising" of ethnic groups, against a background of massive industrialisation. Against such a backcloth the transition in one generation from sect to denomination seemed to be a plausible hypothesis.

The educational and affective influences of a practice such as the "family altar" are held to be quite specific. Conservative Evangelical homes have a predilection for the King James Authorised Version and respondents were keen to stress how familiarity with the KJV helped with Shakespeare. The New International Version is also commented on. This latter has been translated by a panel of conservative Evangelical scholars and has therefore been accepted by the various Evangelical networks. Evangelical outreach groups currently practising in Ulster would be active in building bridges towards Roman Catholics but would distance themselves from other publicly recognised ecumenical groups. The grounds for such a repudiation would be that ecumenical circles would include clerics who are "unsound" or "modernist" on dogmatic matters such as the Virgin Birth. The most strident articulation of such sentiments would emanate from the Free Presbyterian churches. They have been particularly keen to preserve the use of the KJV in worship, and would dissent from the general Evangelical consensus about the NIV. Dr Paisley is unhappy about the term "propitiation" being replaced by "atoning sacrifice" in the NIV. F. F. Bruce points out in "Tradition Old and New" (1970) that frequently groups of believers "fossilise" their traditions (even believers who repudiate the notion of tradition) at the point where their particular movement was at its acme. The Hutterites of Alberta, for example, reproduce the socio-cultural milieu of sixteenth century

Austria and retain their Germanic form of worship.

The translators of the King James Version were working at a period when there was no ideological threat to the sacred tradition embodied in the canon or rule of St. Vincent of Lerins "quod ubique, quod semper, quod ab omnibus creditum est", a reference, circa 434 AD., of an ecumenical character, to the common Christian tradition, to the deposit of the faith accepted "everywhere, always and by all". It is primarily with this unifying canon in mind that various well known Anglicans such as Selwyn Gummer have seceded to the Roman church because of women's ordination. They feel that the Anglican branch of what they regard as the worldwide Catholic Church viz - the Roman, Orthodox and Anglican communions, should have waited for the whole church to make up its collective mind, in the spirit of St. Vincent. (see Wilson. 1954. p.29.)

The conservative cherishing of such a venerable monuments as the KJV is therefore partly concerned with attitudes to tradition. Scholarly work which involved, for example, J. A. T. Robinson, the late and former Bishop of Woolwich, author of "Honest to God" in 1963, would be viewed as contaminated by his involvement. He was regarded as suspect in terms of doctrine in that in "Honest to God" he had endeavoured to replace the supra-naturalist projection of a Heavenly Father - "up there, out there" with a series of images of depth. Even his arguments for an early date for the gospel of John, posthumously delivered in the Bampton lectures of 1984, which would normally have commended him to a conservative audience, would not have exonerated his previous doctrinal aberrations, as they would have been perceived.

Our interviewee continued:

> I meant that the unbiased comments would come from my parents who were supervising the reading - by that I'm trying to get across to you that they did not try to, the only word that comes to me is brainwashing, they didn't try to force me into any mould - as I think that some of my friends later in life, as we discussed our childhoods, I think some of them were pushed pretty hard to follow their parents, probably in some I was but never when I was too young to make up my own mind.

Clearly this interviewee did not experience undue psychological pressure to conform. From a deconstructionist perspective one might argue that the scriptures being read at the family altar are embedded in a mass of commentaries and dictionaries and concordances and aids to worship; that even if at a Bible reading only the text lies before the reader nevertheless there are tacit assumptions in everyone's mind. Nothing of course happens in a vacuum; one need not go so far as to posit the Ideological State Apparatuses of Althusser (see Jones, 1973, p.63.) to take account of the socio-cultural milieu. It is easier to be a Muslim in Saudi Arabia than in Bradford.

On the other hand Felicity Ann O'Dell (1978) describes how the old Soviet system set itself to produce the "new soviet person" within a Marxist-Leninist socio-cultural framework. It was all very thoroughly done but when the economic and social kettle boiled over there seemed to appear deeper well-springs in the human psyche which were expressed through religious beliefs and ethnic ideologies. Since, arguably, the structures of late capitalism rest on approaches to individualism and personal access to Christian scripture which is a form of individualism then a childhood introduction into this sacred deposit such as is formed by the family altar is a most suitable preparation for living in late capitalist conditions. Our interviewee rebutted the notion of parental indoctrination but perhaps from a functional viewpoint in any given culture socialisation towards a measure of conformity is a prerequisite for social cohesion and order.

In response to a question about bible study habits later in life, such as tackling the Books of Job or Jeremiah over a period of time his response was:

> Very simply, no - Possibly because I am not in my own estimation what I would call 'a student', partly that, and I suppose, partly because, as far as Bible reading is concerned my interests have always lain in more of a general overall picture, with personal interests of course going to some particular subjects but not necessarily to entire books.

This is an insightful response. All of our other "exemplars" were in distinguished positions in professional fields; this was the sole exemplar without a long experience of higher education, having joined his father on the ranch at age fifteen. In material terms, he was probably the most prosperous of the exemplars interviewed, as indicated by the airplane parked outside the ranch house. His approach to Bible study therefore was a more electic one, less "academic" than the others and less redolent of a book-lined study. Again and again our data points to the centrality of the Bible for our twentieth century Puritans, but it is interesting that a less structured approach should characterise in one case a busy Prairies rancher and in another some Pentecostal pupils who were children of "blue collar" workers. A leading Elim pastor had in fact remarked in 1991:

> You won't find (as an academic researcher) what you're looking for in the Elim, it's a working class movement.

There was a certain prescience in what he said in that Elim pupils were the least academic in their approach to Bible study and missionary biography and paradoxically, in view of the pneumatology of their church (its strong doctrine of the Holy Spirit) the most "worldly". On the other hand, it may be that the rancher's thematic/personal interest approach may represent a cognitive style related to a busy outdoor life. Bryan Wilson makes the point in "Sects and Society". (1978.) that aspirations to leadership in churches such as Elim will in the end require the aspirant to master both the Christian scriptures and the particular interpretations cherished in various groups.

In response to a question about missionary biography, the interviewee went on to say that:

> I would have to say a rather minor interest I'm getting the feeling of, that I'd like to get across to you that I would not want to try to reach farther than I can comfortably keep my position. I don't know if you understand what I'm saying but I don't want to try to be so involved in something that I fatigue myself to keep up with it.

Our various questions and prompts relating to missionary topics whether historical or contemporary were designed to explore the extent of reading of missionary biographies and contemporary activities and investigate for academic transfer. The rancher disclaimed any deep interest and did not react in detail to any mention of current Evangelical missionary magazines. Once again the pattern established with the other exemplars did not obtain in this instance. It may be that academic researchers tend to look for things academic and are drawn to academic people, perhaps bypassing the active and busy entrepreneur who is not a "bookish" kind of person and perhaps so committed to and involved with business that his interest in the missionary outreach of his church is less than the average. And yet most Canadian/USA Evangelicals would view "tithing" as a principle to be adhered to where possible, a practice which must yield millions of dollars annually towards the missionary enterprise.

His responses on the topic of vocation were equally unexpected:

> What does make a young person choose a career? Fall down in your lap like that? I think in my case I probably followed my hero who was my Dad ..... times in the grain industry and the cattle industry were pretty good ..... that was the opportunity that came up - I was not well educated, only in a country school where the limit was grade 10 - my Dad just said to me, 'Do you want to go on to school, or do you want to start working for real'?

A common response to questions about vocation came from respondents who said that if convinced of a sense of divine vocation they would have obeyed the call, to wherever in the world. That apart, service and status appeared to be strong factors, particularly in regard to working with people. J. C. Davidson and D. P. Caddell in their discussion "Religion and the Meaning of Work" comment:

> ..... high status workers in human services, whose incomes are derived from taxes, who work full time, and who have high job security are most likely to think of their work as a calling, or if they have a more secular world view, a career. Lower status, white-collar employees and blue-collar workers

with part-time jobs and little or no job security, who work with material things in the private sector are not encouraged to think of their work in such noble terms and are not rewarded as highly. (Davidson and Caddell, 1994, pp.135, 136.)

Generally, our interviewees from Evangelical backgrounds had had in the terms of the quotation "noble" aspirations and the rancher's responses seemed by comparison practical and pragmatic and not idealistically academic.

The question was then posed as to whether feelings of "being in a minority" would have characterised members of the church. Conservative Christians take very seriously the New Testament concept of "being ambassadors for Christ" (2 Corinthians 5:20 AV) and thus eschew professional or social linkages in which theoretical principles might be compromised or "heavenly citizenship" (Hebrews 3:1 AV) be marred by practices impairing Christian witness. Strictly interpreted, such teachings imply refraining from the use of alcohol, attending theatres or dances. Also in the Evangelical world at large endogamy would be advised and texts such as Amos 3:3 AV would be frequently cited:

Can two walk together, except they be agreed?

The reply was:

I think you're right when you say it's maybe not as large a question in Canada as where you come from and of course I know nothing of Great Britain, but as you said that I thought and probably even more so because this is rural Canada, because I find here that a particular group of people, and when I say group I mean that they belong to some organisation or church, they are judged not so much on their church but on what kind of character they are in the district because in a rural setting your reputation and your character are well and widely known.

This reply reflects strongly the Canadian emphasis on cultural and religious diversity, in relation, for example, to the rights of "first nations" or smaller religious groups such as the Mennonites. It is evident in Canadian High Schools where the curriculum involves teaching of the mosaic concept of Canada. In contrast, minority religious groups in the UK are likely to experience polite or impolite condenscension (see Horton Davies, 1954) in their deviation from mainline orthodoxy. In Evangelical pulpits in northern Ireland the verse 2 John:10 AV:

If there come any unto you and bring not this doctrine, receive him not into your house neither bid him Godspeed.

is often used in advising that doorstep Mormons and Jehovah's Witnesses are brusquely dismissed, but in North America perceptions would seem not to differentiate between such visitors and the local vicar or priest. North American religious minorities do not appear to feel condescended to or patronised. Commenting on this Bryan Wilson argues that:

> In practice, it is the liberal, democratic, *secular* states such as the United States and Japan, which manifest the greatest degree of tolerance. Liberal democracies in which there is there is an established or a privileged religion, are, for various reasons, just a little less tolerant, and here one might list Britain, Sweden and France. (Wilson, 1990, pp.29-30.)

The Canadian headteacher

The second "exemplar" interview in North America was conducted with a retired headmistress of an elementary school in the Okanagan valley in British Columbia. She had become a well known figure in her community to the extent that when a new school was opened owing to the rapid expansion and development of the Kelowna-Westbank townships, it was named after her. The interview framework was adapted to explore not only her own reflections on her Evangelical childhood but also to elicit her comments about the childhood home, school and church experiences of the sizeable proportion of Evangelical children who had attended the school over the years.

Patterns of demography in parts of Canada have sometimes thrown up significant religio-ethnic concentrations, for example, Eastern Orthodox Slavic in mid-Saskatchewan - Scots/English/Irish Protestant in mid-British Columbia and the Westbank-Kelowna complex has had a substantial Evangelical component of population throughout its development, as evidenced in "From a Log Cabin" 1994 by E. A. Gorman.

In the opening phase of the interview she was invited to reflect on whether past pupils from Evangelical homes had seemed to her to benefit from having come to school from a background that was perhaps relatively structured and therefore physically and emotionally secure and if such practice was general. Her response was:

> It was, yes, not as much in later years, as at the beginning, probably, of my teaching career, but it definitely was very noticeable at the beginning of it. Nearly all of the children that I had came from homes like that; as I taught larger classes there'd be more that came from broken homes where they didn't have that.

Assuming that a teaching career spans a period of approximately forty years this seems to constitute testimony for social change over time. Referring to this type of erosion of former values Bryan Wilson comments:

Yesterday's essentials become today's optionals, lingering as badges of identity which connote a denominational structure, the primary strengths of which may have cause to be group kinship networks, insulating devices and separate institutional support systems. (B. Wilson, 1990, p.12.)

Over time, a Protestant Evangelical ethos may have become diluted; the extended family becomes the nuclear family and the nuclear family becomes the broken family and then the institution of the family comes into question. Liberal interpretations of Christianity have been able to interpret the basic teachings so as to admit "flower-power" type communal living, or to accommodate modifications of the nuclear family pattern in such a way as to tolerate gay couples adopting and rearing children but Evangelicals are always going to be tied to scripture, literally interpreted. A typical New Testament vignette would be I Timothy 3:2-4 NIV:

Now the overseer must be above reproach, the husband of but one wife (there might have been converts from polygamous situations although generally speaking polygamy was rare in the Graeco-Roman world: author), temperate, self-controlled, respectable, hospitable, able to teach, not given to much wine, not violent but gentle, not quarrelsome, not a lover of money. He must manage his own family well and see that his children obey him with proper respect.

Such was the advice for father and children but what of wives and mothers? Evangelicals also are fond of quoting Proverbs 31:15 AV:

She riseth also while it is yet night, and giveth meat to her household, and a portion to her maidens.

Socio-culturally, therefore, when the family unit is encountered whether it be Old Testament or New, it is the extended family which is set out as the "ideally" normal.

The debate about which facets of life, as portrayed in the New Testament, are culturally conditioned and which point to absolute principles is a vigorous one, as instanced currently by the Anglican-Roman tensions over women priests. This is also the case in relation to gender-stereotyping as it affects exclusive religious groups. The Hutterites and Mennonites who, unlike the Amish, have accepted modern technologies, have experienced tensions with regard to gender. Hutterite girls have acquired, in some cases, the necessary keyboard skills much more rapidly than boys. The unforeseen result has been that elders have placed girls in supervisory positions over boys contrary to their beliefs and social norms.

In this connection it may be pertinent to observe that there are mainline Presbyterian congregations in Northern Ireland in whose Sunday schools teenage girls may not teach boys over the age of 11, on the basis of the Pauline injunction in 1 Timothy 2:12 AV[3]:

> But I suffer not a woman to teach, nor to usurp authority over the man, but to be in silence.

The sorts of Evangelical home backgrounds adverted to by the headmistress would have been of the traditional extended or more recent but firmly structured nuclear types, with gender stereotypical role distribution. In response to a question about Bible reading and memorisation of long scriptural passages she replied:

> Some of them, there were some children that would have learned whole chapters, one particular boy that I can think of, he would have learned most of the books of the Bible and in some houses the children would read the Bible with their parents, they also had a system in quite a few of the homes that they read little cards which came from boxes of verses from the Bible and they had to give ... say where they came from in the Bible I remember the same boy, he was really a good student but he was at somebody else's place and they had a box of cards and after the evening meal they passed these cards around and they said, 'What's the matter, why didn't you get that one?' and he said, 'That isn't the box I was brought up on'. He had a wonderful memory.

This is eloquent testimony to a biblicist oral and literary culture as late as mid-twentieth century. The rote learning of passages of scripture in the Authorised Version may not have stimulated educationally desirable goals such as critical autonomy, but at least it will have served to lodge in long term memory tracts of Elizabethan prose and poetry. Even those who were disinclined to see any particular transfer of learning were prepared to agree that exposure to and working with the King James' version put one at an advantage when Shakespeare or Chaucer cropped up in the English curriculum, whether in terms of comprehension of the language at one level or recognising allusions to the King James' version at another.

It is well known that with the decline in religiosity in the United Kingdom many English departments in British universities are providing courses which are introductions to the Bible as literature, to its language, particularly in the older versions and to its literary usages. Conservative Christian worship also, in the collective sense, is thoroughly informed and permeated by the language of the King James or Revised versions. Such worship ranges from the austere simplicities associated in the last century with such believers as the Auld Licht, Anti-Burger, Non-Lifters (followers of the "Old Light", non oath-taking, refusers to lift the bread and the wine at the prayer of consecration) to Sunday morning "Family Services", to Baptist or Assemblies of God services where organ, piano and instrumental music would figure prominently. But right across this liturgical range the Bible, especially in the antique versions, would retain its central position. Although the tele-evangelists of North America are adept at mass communication techniques with their attendant "showbiz" razzamatazz the central feature of each programme will be based on an exposition of the Word.

In settler ideologies it is not simply the linguistic form which is important but also the ideological content which is being mediated via religious observance. Legitimation is provided for the "story" of the people, for their "myth", using the term in its technical sense. The study, reading, recitation and the celebration of the Old Testament narratives also function as the means of recurrently drawing on potent images and symbols. There is, for example, the Exodus motif, the Wandering in the Wilderness motif, the Conquest and Taming of the Territory motif, the expulsion of the Canaanites motif, all of which must have been sources of deep spiritual comfort in the never-ending struggle to tame the wilderness and its inhabitants. The Bible served as a fertile source in the construction of the "story" of the people. The Israelites never forgot the tragedy of Beth-Shan when the ancient foe, the Philistines, swept to victory against Israel, killing Saul's sons and provoking him to fall on his sword, and then, in the custom of the time, dishonouring and exhibiting the bodies on the walls of Beth-Shan. I Samuel 31:12 AV states:

> All the valiant men arose, and went all night, and took the body of Saul and the bodies of his sons from the wall of Beth-Shan, and came to Jabesh and burnt them there.

A signal defeat, later signally avenged.

In 2 Samuel 22:38 David, having triumphed over all his foes, says:

> I have pursued mine enemies and destroyed them, and turned not again till I had consumed them.

The constant reading of such passages and reflection upon them "fed into" the frontier ideology of the settlers and with the exception of groups such as the Quakers instilled a warlike spirit.

The Sioux and the other Indian tribes paid dear for their victory at the battle of the Little Big Horn in Montana, June 25th, 1876.

It must be remembered of course that Evangelicalism resembles a patchwork quilt. Parts of it are, as previously noted, always have been, pacifist, and have often acted against the tide of conquest ideology. The Amish, the Hutterites, the Mennonites, the Quakers,[4] the Needed Truth Brethren have all refused to bear arms. But with regard to North America in general J C Soper observes:

> In America Evangelicalism became the dominant religious perspective by the middle decades of the nineteenth century ...... Evangelical doctrine was

so pervasive by that time that a de facto "common-core Protestantism" had emerged which was nearly synonymous with Evangelical theology. (Soper, 1994, p.46)

Vast numbers and vast movements are involved and vis à vis this mass Evangelicalism it is possible to argue from a secular point of view, as Gusfields's status theory does:

> that Evangelicals were motivated to act on alcohol (ie - in the drive towards Prohibition) because they perceived a threat to their social status with the influx of immigrants at the turn of the century. This threatened social status provided the grassroots' Evangelical support for a movement which wanted to impose prohibition laws in order to codify Evangelical status. (Ibidem, 1994, p.89.)

In reply to a question about music in the Evangelical way of life and Evangelical pupils playing instruments she said;

> Well, some of them had never been used to it, and I don't really know, it might have helped, had they had, but, in later years, they were more involved in music, and I think it did help, but in the early days of teaching very few of them had much contact with music.

The comments above probably reflect practice that has evolved over the span of forty to fifty years in response to rising prosperity and developing musical technologies. In the spirit of evangelists such as W P Nicholson of the 1920's, television and radios would once have been taboo, as purveyors of worldliness into believing homes, but even in the strictest of circles it would seem that the radio has gained acceptance partly because cars all came equipped with radio and cassette player. It may be also that as televisions are progressively miniaturised to wrist watch size they too will gain near universal Evangelical acceptance.

The headmistress came from a background where music would have been absent from worship. Evangelicals in this respect divide along Calvin-Luther emphases - as previously noted Calvin sanctioned only what is specifically mentioned in the New Testament whereas Luther permitted that which was not explicitly forbidden.[5] To this day the Reformed Presbyterians use a tuning fork, without organ or instrumental music, and a precentor raises the psalm. They also regard hymns as manmade constructs and would argue that the word "hymn" in the New Testament connotes only psalms from the Hebrew Psalter. As a result they would restrict themselves to the psalms. But even where instrumental music is eschewed in church worship our findings suggest that it bulks large in the extra-church social backgrounds.

Evangelical book and music shops in Northern Ireland are well stocked with banks of cassettes of all kinds of Evangelical music from Christian "rock" to Handel's Messiah. Interestingly, in North America, the verb "sing" has been transposed into a noun as well. A "sing" is a supper party held at an adherent's house, or in the church basement, after the Sunday evening meeting, where people gather round the piano or organ or guitars and spend an hour singing the old classical "Wesleys" and "Watts" and the more modern choruses and hymns of "Mission Praise". Alternatively, in times of good weather, a sing may be held at a barbecue at the beach or lake-side to the accompaniment of accordion, guitars and mouth-organs. The importance of instrumental music to the socialising outside of church means that Evangelical children often learn two instruments. As the interviewee commented in reference to instrumental tuition:

> They do, in the High School here, to begin with, when I lived here, there was no music taught at all, now they have a band they learn all these instruments. My nieces and nephews that are going to school now, from almost grade one up, are all interested in learning some kind of musical instrument.

There is a venerable tradition in Evangelicalism of the composition of lively hymns, although they also cherish ancient hymns they like, such as "St Patrick's Breastplate" composed by Patrick in the 5th century, or "Jesus the Very Thought of Thee, with Sweetness fills my breast, But sweeter far Thy face to see, And in Thy presence rest", by Bernard of Clairvaux in the 12th century. The "lively" tradition runs back to the Wesleys in the 18th century, Cowper, Watts and Bonar being writers of more sombre words and melodies, and received an extra emphasis when General Booth of the Salvation Army declared that the devil should not have a monopoly over good tunes. But apart from "Sings" at Sunday evening parties well played music is important to Evangelicals because of the notion of "witness". Luke shows the Risen Jesus saying to his disciples in Acts 1:8:

> But you will receive power when the Holy Spirit has come upon you and you will be my witnesses in Jerusalem, and, in all Judea and Samaria and as far as the end of the earth. (Translation by author)

"Bearing witness".. (Greek - martur¢ew) is a concept dear to Evangelical hearts and frequently takes the place of an open-air meeting. Very often bright and lively choruses will be sung in order to hear the exposition of the Word. Musical talent is therefore at a premium and can be just as important to attract an audience within the church as the more common oral tradition of sermons. Amongst Pentecostals, whether "classical" Pentecostalists, looking back to the Azusa St. Mission revival of 1906 in North America or the Reverend A. Boddy and the accompanying ecstatic phenomena in Europe in the early 1900's or neo-

Pentecostalist charismatics looking back to the Episcopalian and Catholic experiences of the sixties in mid-west USA, music has always been of prime importance in both worship and witness. The tendency amongst them is to form orchestras in their churches, accompanied by formally dressed choirs. In the interests of witness some Evangelical churches have transferred the "breaking of bread" service from Sunday morning to a weekday evening and have devoted Sunday mornings to "family services". The motive is evangelistic in the belief that the unchurched fathers and mothers in a neighbourhood are perhaps most likely on a Sunday morning to react positively to an invitation to come to church "en famille", and participate in worship and song, and hear scripture expounded. Some stricter Evangelicals object to this partly on scriptural grounds , in that we read in Acts 20:7 NIV:

> "On the first day of the week we came together to break bread" (Paul and the Eutychus incident at Troas),

and this is considered scriptural precedent for holding the communion service on Sunday mornings, and partly on the grounds of seemliness, namely that Sunday morning family service had come to be like a night-club. Such a charge is perhaps more credible in a North American setting where churches are carpeted, have cinema-type seating, electric organs, stages with microphones, saxophonists, soloists, etc., although this type of church architecture and furniture can increasingly be found in the UK. In the case, particularly, of the house-church movement, as it has expanded, it has found that houses cannot accommodate numbers and it has tended to buy up properties such as cinemas, auction halls and the like and to decorate them inside with plush fittings. Alternatively a growing and burgeoning church may build a vast new building with accommodation for orchestra, choir, etc and soft seating. Examples in Belfast would be the suburban Glenmachan Church of God (East) or at the other end of the city, the Metropolitan Tabernacle, both vast auditoria in the American style.

When the interview moved on to the topic of missionary biography and whether her charges were familiar with it she replied:

> I think that there are a great many of those ones in the books that would be on the missionaries, especially Evangelical missionaries, a few maybe of the other books of more recent years, some of the older ones like to extend their reading a little bit more largely because of travel they are very interested in some of these other countries, but missionary books have always been taught ...... the children of today travel a lot more than the children did twenty or thirty years ago.

It can be gathered from this reply that the school library and the homes of her Evangelical pupils had been, as expected, well stocked with missionary biographies. She also adds that there had been an interest in Christian missionary work in general, outside of specifically Evangelical circles. Perhaps she had in mind organisations such as Christian Aid. She also mentions most interestingly increasing travel. The traditional missionary departed from the quayside to the soulful strains of:

> God be with you till we meet again,
> By His counsels guide, uphold you,
> With His sheep securely fold you,
> God be with you till we meet again..
> Till we meet, till we meet,
> Till we meet at Jesus' feet, etc.
> (Ira D. Sankey, 1982, No.298)

He or she would have expected to be absent from the home base for at least five years. Like Paul and Barnabus in Acts 13 they were commended to the unknown. When they returned on furlough, like Paul and Barnabas, "they reported all that God had done through them". (Acts 14:27 NIV).

This somewhat Victorian pattern has begun to change in the past thirty years because of the greater prosperity of people living in western industrialised societies and the relative cheapness of air travel. Many Evangelical Christians who take an interest in, regularly pray for and financially support missionaries abroad have, where feasible, been going to visit them. With affordable travel missionaries and their families now commute to the homeland more often. The concept of diversification has also arrived. This entails that a missionary vocation may not be life-long, but might end after a decade, when the worker returns home for the sake of the children's education. Short period terms abroad have also been encouraged in many churches, particularly for relief purposes where a nurse or a doctor or engineer may go out to a specific location for 2 years, then return home. "Echoes of Service" (June 1994) which carries news of some missionaries of the Christian Brethren, lists 14 names giving short-term help overseas of 2 months or more. The target countries are India, Zaire, Zimbabwe, Pakistan, Lebanon, Germany and Zambia.

Another factor involved with the facility of travel is that personnel from abroad, converts of the missionary effort, or children or grandchildren of converts may elect to come and visit the home churches or they may be businessmen brokering deals or academics taking up visiting fellowships. This is not necessarily an unmixed blessing for the churches and missionaries involved; they may inadvertently have given the impression abroad that the homeland is a serenely Christian country and then find that the foreign Christians are appalled at the materialism, the inner city decay, the vagrancy and the homelessness.

A further factor facilitating a certain amount of interchange is the nationalisation of assets and suchlike developments. Evangelical missionary work has generally advanced on two fronts, the preaching of the Word and the building of clinics and hospitals. It has always been a black and white effort, with its clearcut set of priorities, and would never, as with Roman Catholic missions, have been accused of syncretism with indigenous cultures. But as country after country gained independence and set in motion development plans, hospital buildings, built under mission auspices, were nationalised. The governments, however, usually did not want to lose the consultants, the doctors, the nurses, and in the case of schools, the teachers and frequently offered them contracts to remain as state employees. This involves receipt of salary and regular vacations, with the regular opportunity to return home. Very often also the "terms" on which nationalisation of assets has taken place have been favourable to missionaries in a general sense, because the leaders of various nations received their early education in mission schools. Two examples would be Kenneth Kaunda and Julius Nyerere. Hostility is sometimes experienced in places and tensions arise. The Brazilian government, for example, runs an Institute of Indian Linguistics in Sao Paulo, whose task it is to discover, describe, translate and write grammars for the multitudinous Indian languages of the Matto Grosso. The professional linguists and anthropologists employed in this task generally try to leave the Indian cultures concerned in the equipoise they have achieved with their jungle environments and look askance at the interventionist approach of Christian missions.

As the interview drew to a close the topic arose of the nearness in time of the frontier spirit, of the famed Prairies, and far west hospitality. The interviewee replied:

> You see, the country is so much younger. The country was only twenty years old when my mother was born, in 1887. 1867 was the confederation - she was born in Ontario. It seems to be done that way in Canada (hospitality).

The frontier spirit is celebrated in books such as those written by Janette Oke. Typically a story may begin with the wagon train and the staking of a claim and with the building of a flourishing Prairie town. The Old Testament conquest motif is resonant in such stories. Sometimes the heroes and heroines return back east and become corrupted, as they savour "the fleshpots of Egypt" (Exodus 16:3 AV). Amongst Evangelicals the frontier ideal, particularly with regard to women, seems remarkably durable in the face of modernity. Even in the neighbourhood of vast supermarkets, bottling, canning, baking bread, are still characteristic of many homes. Where these arts and skills are in danger of being forgotten church groups and extra-mural college and university departments lay on courses for the local womenfolk. In terms of hospitality, when guests arrive the delights of the cellar are broached. And just as in the last century the cellar in winter was literally a "deep-freeze" nowadays a large electrically operated deep-freeze will usually stand next to the cellar.

The veterinary surgeon

The third exemplar interview conducted in North America was with a veterinary surgeon who had a large practice on the southern Canadian prairies and so near the frontier with the USA that the family crossed over to shop for food and petrol.

The interview began with a question about the influence of the interlocking nexus of home, school and church factors on academic achievement in childhood and quickly centred on the reading of scripture:

> The effect of reading the scriptures, I'm fully convinced that it had some effect on my ability to read in school because we always read the scriptures out loud at home and that got a lot of new words into our vocabulary and we were able to read books of a more difficult nature than a lot of the other students at school.

It can be taken as read that the Bible was once again being read aloud around the table in the KJV. This is a further example of children from Evangelical families growing up and from earliest days being saturated in the English of Tyndale and Coverdale, and in the Hebraic and Greek thought-forms that lay behind them. Two particular factors are mentioned in the response: the ever increasing vocabulary and the advanced reading ability when school was attended.

If we were to generalise from our exemplars we should be positing large numbers of Evangelical children who were near prodigies in school, precocious in their ability to grapple with Shakespeare and Dickens and knowledgeable about history and geography. And yet the overall picture would not bear out such an expectation. Steve Bruce (1989, p.187.) cites an American survey which alludes to the strong correlation between liberalism and education. The study indicated that, of the population surveyed, 14.4% of liberal Christians had completed university as opposed to 8.9% of Evangelicals. The distinction between liberal and Evangelical is the broadest one employed in this book and effectively includes in the Evangelical fold essentially those who would have espoused the classic American "Fundamentals": the infallibility of scripture, the Virgin Birth, the substitutionary atonement, the bodily Resurrection and physical Second Coming of Jesus. It may be that in overall terms those who accept this corpus of dogma and affirm the New Birth are under-represented in higher education, at least in North America.

In order, however, to obtain as clear a focus as possible our research focused on near 'ideal-typical' Evangelicals, those who not only accepted a core set of

Evangelical beliefs but who also tended to see the borders between the profane and the sacred in very non-sacramental or non-traditional liturgical terms. It may be that in this particular sub-group of Evangelicals as a whole the distribution of high achievers is greater. Certainly Weber, as already observed, drew attention to the particularly rapid upward social mobility of groups such as Quakers (most non-sacramental of all) and Mennonites.

The interview then moved on to the topic of whether personal Bible study was systematic or not. The reply was:

> I would say it was when I was in first year university, when I was out on my own, it was then, yeah, when I was at home I would read the Bible but as far as getting into it in any depth it wasn't until first year university.

It is natural that an undergraduate settling into rooms in university should make "all things new", and begin a new regime of Bible-study. It transpired that systematic study entailed taking the New Testament books one by one and then at a later stage those of the Old Testament.

In the Canadian system aspirant doctors and veterinarians do a degree in science before advancing to specific medical or veterinary studies. So the interviewee was referring to a first year course centring on chemistry and biology, with possibly some physics and mathematics. Grappling with the Hebrew/Aramaic or the Greek in the evenings or early mornings must have substantially broadened the epistemological base. Not that formal learning of Hebrew/Aramaic or Greek would be involved, but at this level of adult study Evangelical commentaries engage the student in transliterated Hebrew and Greek terms, and their precise shade of meaning, so that a vocabulary of words and phrases would be acquired. In this process not only commentaries on individual books would be used, such as the Tyndale Commentary on Romans by F. F. Bruce, but also works such as W. E. Vine's Expository Dictionary of New Testament words. To cite a particular example from Vine the last entry on page 252 reads:

> E. SULLOGIZOMAI (sullog¢izomai), to compute (sun, with, and logizomai; (cp. Eng. syllogism)) also denotes to reason, and is so rendered in Luke 20:5 AV.

Thus the seriously inclined Evangelical student begins to develop a kind of Biblical "pidgin" Hebrew and Greek. For some, this interest will inevitably lead to a study of the textual traditions underlying the various Biblical manuscripts, and the Bible student inducts himself into the whole world of vellum codices, i.e. manuscripts in book format, with the leaves made of dried skin, such as Codex Sinaiticus in the British Museum and of papyri. This study will involve the acquisition of a whole new vocabulary - uncials (manuscripts printed in capital letters by scribes) minuscules (MSS in cursive, small letter script), textus receptus, i.e. the Received or Byzantine Text from which the KJV was translated and so forth. In view of the intellectual territory, both biblical and extra biblical, which the Evangelical student begins to cover in daily systematic study one can appreciate that at times the dialogue with liberal Christian laymen can be fraught. The educated Evangelical student tends to be an expert, relatively speaking, on matters biblical and para-biblical and the mainline layman, even if an elder of a mainline church, should argument arise, may have to go to his minister for help or information, whereas the Evangelical is a kind of DIY theologian. Sometimes also the smaller Christian groupings are augmented by people of an Evangelical and spiritual bent who are more at home there, with the intense study of and discussion of the bible, than in the more nominal practice of the main-line church. Even within the Evangelical fold gradations are made and one may hear, colloquially put, in Ulster, accounts such as that:

> He left the Brethren to go into the Elim, but the Elim were "light in the Word", so he ended up in the Baptists. (anecdotally related to one of the authors)

It may seem at first blush surprising that as large and variegated a body of people as constitute the Evangelical world should develop such wide-ranging expertise in matters biblical but our research has shown how at the age of sixteen or seventeen adolescents are setting aside a time each day to study and meditate on passages of scripture, with concomitant aids. Where it is possible to do so, Evangelical young people take up the study of Greek, and no doubt, were Hebrew available, would opt for it also. The "exemplar" figures interviewed are all in positions in career and life where they can turn their formidable talents towards bible-centred and ancillary studies and one is not surprised that they begin to evince the sure-footed approach to the bible of the professional theologian.

The research indicated that adolescent Evangelicals were heavily involved in a diverse range of church related activities; a major part of which in all probability centred on the bible and Christian moral perspectives. As such young people pass into adulthood they are going to advance into positions of leadership in churches, the diaconate, the eldership, the select vestry, lay preaching, and will continue to extend and deepen their biblical and theological perspectives. Or if they choose to proceed along the "Evangelical network" path and to become heavily involved in Evangelical organisations such as Scripture Union or Crusaders or TEAR fund or Leprosy Mission support work they will be working in situations where biblical knowledge is highly valued as the underpinning of a world-view. The converse of this is that positions of seniority and leadership in the Evangelical world are only open to those who have mastered the basics of the Christian faith as evangelically interpreted.

Negative conclusions may be and are drawn about the whole matter of the bible and the intellectual mastery of it. From a Marxist perspective Christopher Hill writes:

> The Bible lost its universal power once it had been demonstrated that you could prove anything from it, and that there was no means of deciding once the authority of the church could not be enforced (How right Rome had been!). Hobbe's attempt to substitute secular authority failed. Fragmentation - both intellectual and of congregations - was one of the most important consequences of religious toleration. Many still continued to believe that truth could and should be found in the Bible but could not agree on what it was (we may compare the devastating consequences of the abolition of the authoritative position of the Communist Party and its ideology in eastern Europe in 1989-90). The Bible became a historical document, to be interpreted like any other. Today its old authority exists only in dark corners like Northern Ireland or the Bible Belt of the USA. (C. Hill, 1993, p.428.)

Such an evaluation as the above would not commend itself to Evangelicalism worldwide. The interview then moved on to Hebrew and Greek in detail, and mention was made of a "library" of theological/biblical works lining the study wall. The reply was:

> I haven't really got into the Hebrew but I had bought that group of books from an old gentleman but as far as the Greek I had some Greek books before that and it (the study of Greek) would go back maybe to 1975, when I started that.

The story is told by F. F. Bruce, (1950, p.10) of John Nelson Darby, one of the main founders of the movement that came to be known as the Plymouth Brethren, that when he had seceded from the Church of Ireland to pursue an itinerant preaching ministry, he resolved to give away his possessions. He was uncertain however whether this resolve should include his library and felt that he had received guidance to retain the collection because at the particular time he was studying 2 Corinthians Chapter 4, of which the thirteenth verse reads:

> As for the cloak, which I left behind at Troas with Carpus, bring it with you when you come, and the books as well, especially the parchments.

Darby related this story in connection with an enquiry as to whether believers in the 19th century could find relevant guidance in every verse of scripture, including those of an ephemeral significance, his answer being affirmative. Many Evangelicals would accumulate just such a specialist library, of books relating to the Bible, Theology and Church history.

Evangelical bookshops cater for such a market. Apart from the "modern" Evangelical output, Tyndale Commentaries, apologetics by distinguished leaders such as John Stott of All Souls College Oxford, Langham Place and the like, the shelves are stocked with books by the great conservative scholars and preachers of Victorian and Edwardian times - Charles Handley Moule, The Princeton Theologians, B. B. Warfield and C. Hodge, and with biographies of the Founding Fathers of Evangelical Foreign Mission, Hudson Taylor and C. T. Studd and others.

The interview moved on from discussion of the specifically Biblical library to a consideration of what Bourdieu calls "habitus", attitude to books and to study. The reply was:

> Yes, because of not having television in the home and spending the time watching it we developed more of an aptitude for books and other things to pass our time which had a very positive effect rather than a negative effect on us.

There is a spectrum of Evangelical attitudes to the accoutrements of the modern world. Some, as noted, remain apparently fossilised at the acme of their development, such as the Hutterites, who allow a modicum of modern technology, but not television, except for teachers from outside living on the Bruderhof. To be a practising member of the Assemblies of God (a Pentecostal Church numbering 15,000,000 adherents in the USA), you are required to state in writing that you abstain from such practices as smoking, drinking alcohol, going dancing and the like. The impression gained however is that the tide of modernity is "on the flow", and that those individual Evangelicals who eschew it are in a clear minority. In discussion with such groups the view will be advanced that one cannot compare North American TV with British and the comment is often made that it would be a different matter to decide if BBC2 and Channel 4, say, in the United Kingdom were under discussion. But in a situation where 14 channels are available, 13 of which are of low artistic value, and constantly interrupted by unheralded advertising, some Evangelicals adopt the austere practice of abstention, with the exception that perhaps at weekends they will hire out a video and a video-player and show a film on the VDU at their computer.

Evangelicals in general are strongly family orientated. Soper (1994) notes that one of the main planks in the Evangelical campaigns against pornography, such as that known as the Festival of Light, rests on the fact that pornography promotes non-family values. Where Evangelicals do possess televisions it is probably the case that children's viewing is strictly controlled. The interviews with pupils revealed a spectrum of Northern Irish practice in this regard ranging from "no television" in the home through parental control to no overt control but parental trust in the adolescents to switch off when appropriate.

Next, the question of music was explored, with particular reference to it as a factor in the Evangelical worldview and as to whether or not Evangelicals preferred classical secular music. The response was:

> Yes, I do, I think, and that goes back to our times at home when often times, after having a Bible reading, we'd sit and sing and sing with no accompaniment, but just sing and sing with no accompaniment, but just sing and it was - it gave me an appreciation for good musical times - I've never had a liking for the modern jazz or the rock music or that type of thing .... yeah, Handel's Messiah I have that in .... I like Bach ....

The interviewee graduated from High School to University in the mid-seventies, so his reflections as to music encompass a time when serious modern approaches to hymnody such as that represented by hymnals such as "Mission Praise" had not appeared, nor composers such as Graham Kendrick. So the hymns he grew up with would have been dominated by Watts, Doddridge, the Wesleys, Toplady, Alexander, Bonar, Newton, Havergal, Rossetti, Cowper, Zinzendorf, Baxter, and others who composed at the apogee of Evangelical hymnody.

So it came as no surprise that a musical taste formed in such circumstances would be one that favoured Bach and Handel. One interesting document which met the eye in a home similar to that of the vet was a "key" to Handel's Messiah in verse-by-verse terms so that:

> "Comfort ye" on the left was accompanied by, on the right, the note Isiaih 40:1-3

> "I know that my Redeemer liveth" read across to Job 19:25-26 + 1 Corinthians 15:20.

It would seem that the Messiah in particular is the locus of a perfect fusion of music and scripture.

Asked about missionary biography and interest he replied:

> Yes, like C. T. Studd, I remember reading him, David Livingstone, there's others too well, it certainly gave me some idea about Africa. We get "Horizons" (a missionary magazine) and of course it's got articles in there from Chile, Malawi, China, Hong Kong and so all over.

In general terms it would seem clear that as Evangelical children and adolescents grow up they are exposed to the "Roll of Honour" of the pioneer missionaries. One of our teacher colleagues in Northern Ireland had been brought up on the mission field and nurtured on tales of the pioneers. She had been educated until the age of ten by correspondence courses, which her mother had supervised. At ten she had begun to attend the local (Spanish-speaking school); by 9 1/2, however, she had read all there was to read about Hudson Taylor, Geraldine Taylor and the Guinness connection, the Cambridge Seven, Fox's Book of Martyrs and other "exemplar" type books. Such precocious literacy is fostered of course against a background of a primitive native culture, without radio, without television, and being kept indoors when the great South American fiestas such as "Mardi Gras" were taking place. She related how when she went to university and read History she realised with a shock that the Boxer rising of 1902 in China was not in fact the world-shattering event that the China Inland literature had portrayed it as.

The interview then moved on to consider the notion of vocation:

> When I was in High School they were wondering, well, what does the Lord really want me to do, but, I mean, if He wants me to be a missionary, I'd certainly be willing to go, but that avenue didn't open up at any time but it gave me something to do, to realise that you know, God has some purpose for me and whatever it is it was certainly in High School when veterinary medicine caught my eye and if the Lord didn't want me to go to some mission field that's where I'd like to be, type of thing.

As with all our Evangelical interviewees/respondents there is evidence here of an impressive sense of willingness to serve God wherever, whenever the person may be "called". The interviewees seem to have considered the possibility that there might be a divine vocation to missionary service whether in terms of full-time service abroad or of taking a job abroad so as to be of assistance to a foreign church. Evangelicals have often been criticised for their lack of emphasis on social work and indeed the neo-Evangelicals in the USA have almost become a separate party with a social work emphasis, in contrast to those whom they designate as fundamentalists. In the United Kingdom, similarly, the activities of TEAR fund (The Evangelical Alliance Relief fund) have steadily expanded in the last twenty years and have enjoyed general Evangelical support. Against the charge of social quietism, however, must be laid the general Evangelical missionary record which is one of self-sacrifice, of building hospitals, clinics and schools, of spreading literacy and numeracy. Individual missionary societies, as previously noted, such as the "New Tribes" mission have drawn the fire of opponents on the grounds that they destroy the native cultures, of, say, the Latin American indigenous tribes and turn them into camp-followers of the mission station and subsequently, when they are pacified and westernised, into cheap labour. Perhaps it may be inevitable that across the spectrum of missionary endeavour different emphases are visible. A particular group whose centre of gravity is American Bible-belt fundamentalism may in fact be mediating late capitalist values in a radical way. The interface between cultures is hardly going to be free of friction when a neolithic or hunter-gatherer peoples encounter late capitalism. In New Guinea such a meeting occasioned the rise of cargo cults, because the gap between the perceptions of the world of the tribes-people and that of the newcomers was such a pronounced one that real communication between the two groups yielded to a species of awe.

Evangelical missionaries of course feel themselves to be bound by the Matthaean Great Commission Mt 28:19 AV:

> Go ye therefore, and teach all nations, baptising them in the name of the Father, and the Son, and the Holy Ghost.

When they are accused of ideological colonisation they would tend to argue that, in the case of primitive societies and cultures, the obligation to combat disease and ignorance and to promote literacy and numeracy are over-riding imperatives. They would regard the gradualist Jesuit efforts in South America as syncretising.

A question was then posed to the effect that, when a missionary vocation did not eventuate, was the chosen veterinary career decided on because of financial implications. The reply was:

> No, no. To make a good living, yes, to provide for my family, but as far as making big dollars, no. Never entered my head.

This response chimed in with an ethos that would seem to be widespread in the mid-western prairies; the head of the family feels a clear obligation "to put bread on the table", to "provide for the family". Discussions with high school pupils indicated that the curriculum in Canadian secondary schools is "politically correct", anti-racist, anti-gender stereotypes, and anti-ageist. But the old stereotypes are durable and linger on. Most of the Evangelicals interviewed would have been influenced with regard to gender considerations by the New Testament. They would not, as theologians of the Biblical Theology movement would have done, tend to try to extrapolate abiding principles from an historical and socio-cultural setting, arguing that the Pauline teaching about woman's place is temporally conditioned. Evangelicals on the whole would tend to see woman's supportive role and functions as a given datum, that is as a basic part of the world and society as God had created them and meant them to be.

The final phase of the interview centred on the question of whether Evangelicals feel in a minority because of the need to avoid certain social settings and practices. The answer was:

> Yes, I would say yes, when we were growing up we weren't allowed to do many of the things that a lot of our friends were doing in school or go to places where many of them were going and we felt a very distinct minority group amongst them and it didn't matter really an awful lot but because we felt we had God on our side who is far bigger than anybody else so that

116

seemed to make the difference and so what?

For Evangelicals the pivotal verses in this connection would be :

2 Corinthians 6:17 AV

Wherefore come out from among them and be ye separate, saith the Lord, and touch not the unclean thing, and I will receive you.

and :

Romans 14:21 AV

It is good neither to eat flesh, nor to drink wine, nor any thing whereby thy brother stumbleth, or is offended, or is made weak.

As previously observed, a doctrine of separation may be held in a weak or a strong form. Usually the weak form stresses abstention from moral evil; i.e. it is permissible to visit the cinema if a wholesome film is being shown, such as the "Sound of Music", or to participate in dancing at the youth club (but not heavy rock at a disco), whereas a strongly held doctrine inveighs against any attendance at places tainted or contaminated by unacceptable associations. The cinema may be showing the "Sound of Music" this week but last week it showed "Basic Instinct", and furthermore a "weak brother", i.e. a recent convert, unlearned in the faith, might see one going in, and be "caused to stumble". (1 Corinthians 8:9,10 AV). All Evangelicals however would be agreed on "separation to the Lord" in terms of the most serious dimensions of life. Thus an intra-evangelical endogamy is encouraged, not along denominational lines generally, though occasionally so, but along the lines that a person who is saved, born-again, ought to marry an equally saved person, otherwise the marriage constitutes an "unequal yoke", in the words of 2 Corinthians 6:14 AV.[6] Bryan Wilson (1990) argues that the erection of such boundaries functions as a "distancing stratagem" and therefore as a reinforcement to discipline but it would seem also that the boundaries function as demarcators between the sacred and the profane. Samarin (1972) argues that the practice of glossolalia "speaking in tongues" is one which fulfils no intrinsic linguistic functions; the "tongues" when analysed are not foreign languages, but they do function as demarcators of the sacred. It might be observed that the reason for the "disciplinary fencing" is at base the idea that a particular domain is sacred, and needs marked off.

The practice of glossolalia and the other charismata is marking out an area of life wherein the believer is saying "God is active here - This is holy ground" in the same way as the communicant at the eucharist makes a similar statement.

117

Conclusion

The seven interviewees represented a diversity of backgrounds. Five were male, two were female. Given that they had been chosen as leading figures they all had successful professional or business careers behind them, in three instances combining in one persona a variety of career activities. Given again that most successful careers take time to develop the age distribution would have lain approximately between forty and sixty. One had become successful in business life without having had more than rudimentary North American high school experience educationally and one had relinquished the Evangelical faith of childhood. All had been brought up in Evangelical homes, and in that sense, were not converts from a completely different way of life to Evangelicalism, although each would have had an experience of intra-church individual conversion.

The norm for those brought up within an Evangelical home and church background would be that they could identify a definite change in their lives as having taken place, whether it took the form of a sudden Damascus road conversion, as described in relation to Saul of Tarsus in the ninth chapter of Acts, or whether a more gradual and less perceptible spiritual change had been in view. A minority of Evangelicals might express their faith in such a way as to indicate that they do not remember a time at which they did not "love the Lord Jesus".

Geographically the exemplars represent a spread of experience; in British

Columbia, the Prairies, Northern Ireland, the Republic of Ireland, England south and north, Ethiopia, Spain and Eastern Europe, both in terms of upbringing and education and the occupations followed in later life. Ecclesiastically they belong to what is sometimes described as the pietist evangelical tradition. Steve Bruce notes:

> As an aside and for the sake of completeness, it is worth adding that not all evangelicals would have the political involvement of the Paisleyites or those in the main churches who share many of their views. There is in Ulster a *pietistic* evangelical tradition which sees religion as an alternative to the ways of the world and which stresses the importance of avoiding worldly contamination. Especially strong in working-class urban areas, a gospel-hall and Pentecostal tradition serves as a way out of the everyday world and offers an alternative persona and career for many former terrorists. (S. Bruce, 1994, p.35)

Bruce identifies here a constituency within the Evangelical world where the core values and verities of Evangelicalism perhaps shine through more luminously than in other ecclesiastical settings. Leading Ulster Evangelicals who are active in politics and also prominent figures in the mainline churches, such as the Reverend Martyn Smyth, Member of Parliament at Westminster and Presbyterian minister, find themselves within their denominations rubbing shoulders with colleagues of liberal or radical theological views and thereby incurring the charge of theological compromise by association. The concept however of a pietist Evangelical tradition which is quietist in its approach to politics may need to be modified. The Elim church, for example, which would have evinced a separatist ethic and which in the Second World War would have numbered some conscientious objectors amongst its ranks, particularly amongst ministers, was represented at the formation of the Ulster loyalist "Ulster Clubs" in 1986, by a leading pastor, who led the audience in prayer. Steve Bruce remarks of this:

> Peter Robinson and other DUP leaders helped form the Ulster Clubs as a new vehicle to co-ordinate grass-roots protest. (Bruce, 1994, Ibid, p.104.)

It may be that the eschatological views which are cherished in the pietist gospel-hall and Pentecostal tradition, and which impinge on and influence conservative Protestants in mainline churches, afford such a nefarious "prophetic" role to the Roman Catholic church that a shift for some formerly pietist Evangelicals in the Irish situation has taken place towards political activism. Two recently composed hymns sung by a popular and well-known Evangelical singer, Mary McKee, seem to be interpretable in somewhat, for Evangelicals of the pietist tradition, unusual political terms. The lyrics in question are entitled firstly: "No weapon that is formed against thee shall prosper", based on a verse from Isaiah (54:17 AV), and presumably directed against the Anglo-Irish Agreement signed between Margaret Thatcher and Garrett Fitzgerald at Hillsborough in 1985, and abominated by most unionists because the unionist parties were not consulted about it; and secondly: "I will serve no alien god", based on such verses as Psalm 44:20 AV, a hymn perhaps directed against the concept of a United Ireland. Our exemplars, however, despite the possibility of such changes in attitude having taken place would fall fairly firmly into the category of past or present quietist Evangelicalism, save that one of them would be well-known as a hard-hitting radio political commentator of moderate hue.

Despite their disparate backgrounds however they are revealed by the interviews as sharing in a commonalty of biographical features. There appears in the account of each of them the same structured busy home-background, revolving round the twin axes of familial Christian devotion and church activities. School seems to have functioned for all as an extension of this busy pattern of life, and as an area wherein both academic and extracurricular pursuits could be enjoyed and profited from. Their lives were all so filled with these functional practices that little if any room was left for frivolity. Separation from worldly contamination seems rather to have been a consequence of days and evenings filled with activities regarded as wholesome or sanctificatory than of obedience to any formally stated set of separatist values. There would be a contrast in this respect with the practice of some introversionist sects (in Bryan Wilson's classification) such as the Exclusive Brethren, whose children in school are formally withdrawn from any parts of curricula which involve television or computers.

All the exemplars had positive attitudes to family values, particularly as those related to busy childhoods passed in an oscillation between family and home background on the one hand and school on the other. Leisure activities were dominated by reading and by music. One can appreciate how important the foci of social behaviour become to individuals, of home, school and church and how activities deflecting attention away from this tri-focal perspective, such as ski-trips abroad, with their attendant "worldly" après-ski night-life would hold out little allure. (Functional ski-ing in, say, North Alberta, would be differently evaluated).

As each interview wound to a close some reflective discussion arose as to socio-political attitudes and philosophies of life. Only one of the interviewees was active politically, the remaining six would have been of a quietist disposition and would have subscribed to the notion of obedient citizenship in accord with Romans 13:1 AV: "The powers that be are ordained of God", provided that individual religious conscience was not stifled, as in contemporary China, for many believers. This political quietism is accompanied of course by a strong missionary interest, particularly with regard to foreign missions, and a sense of urgency exists with regard to the "fields being white unto harvest"; i.e. the heathen masses waiting to be evangelised as the End draws near. Political interest in world events is keen, particularly in regard to the State of Israel and militant Islam, as both of these are susceptible of interpretation in eschatological categories.

Notes

1. The King James Authorised Version incorporated much of the translation of William Tyndale and Miles Coverdale; the latter's renditions of some of the psalms are particularly felicitous.
2. The adjective "sectarian" here is used in its neutral, sociological sense and not in its common pejorative meaning.
3. It may be that the so-called Pastoral Epistles 1 and 2 Timothy and Titus do not come in their present form from Paul himself, but rather from a Pauline school, writing later F. F. Bruce argues in Peake's Bible Commentary that they

incorporate "disiecta membra" - scattered fragments of Paul's correspondence. Injunctions as to the silence of women in St Paul's work constitute a problem. It is difficult to reconcile 1 Corinthians 11 with 1 Corinthians 14 and the Pastoral Epistles.

4. Briefly, at the beginning of their history, until about 1650, the Quakers were not pacifist.

5. Luther would be generally regarded as having promoted a reformed Catholicism, and so many features of Catholic doctrine and liturgy would have survived relatively unimpaired. Compare the "via media Anglicana".

6. In the opinion of the authors' AV here represents the full force of the Greek, NIV "Do not be yoked together" is a secularising toning down.

5 Theories of secularisation and social movement and Evangelicals

A succinct and eloquent statement of recent secularisation theory is provided by Bryan Wilson:

> Whatever the influences that religious traditions may have exerted on eastern and western cultures in the past, in the modern world there appears to be a virtually universal process in which the social influence of religion diminishes - a process known to sociologists as secularisation. In the differing historical contexts of eastern and western cultures, divergent specific causes have no doubt been active in the precise course by which religion has lost its social significance. The decline of western religion has been associated with the emergence of new and more powerful influences on the shape of western culture, in particular the two agencies that we have already mentioned: the growth of science and the development of the state. It might also be argued that the specific course of religious change itself not only accommodated the nascent tendencies towards a more secular society, but in certain respects also stimulated that process. Protestantism was a reform of Christianity which promoted very considerable rationalisation both of religious ideas and of everyday life. It did so by reducing the plethora of powers to which popular Catholicism subscribed. In its vigorous transcendentalism, it eliminated the remaining immamentist elements that had arrived in the Roman Church. Magical intercessions, special places of holiness, relics, and shrines were all condemned. The magical interpretation of the sacraments was abrogated. Rituals were henceforth to be regarded more as memorials than as acts that manifested intrinsic power. (Wilson, 1982, p.80.)

Wilson chooses his words very carefully in thus outlining secularisation theory. There is ample scope for debate about particular points and in consequence one notes the implicit caveats he lodges in his exposition - "appears to be", "virtually universal", "divergent specific causes", "no doubt", "associated with", "nascent tendencies", "in certain respects", "very considerable rationalisation", are all phrases which carry with them a sort of inbuilt qualification, and indicate the extent to which the theory of secularisation as thus stated may be contested. An up to date full blooded rebuttal is argued by Stark and Iannacone. They comment:

> over the past decade, however, faith in the secularisation thesis has been declining, particularly among sociologists who work in the area of religion - a development of such magnitude that Stephen Warner (1993) (previously cited by authors) has labelled it a shift in scientific paradigms.

They go on to remark:

> It seems clear that the secularisation thesis has been falsified - that the evolutionary future of religion is not extinction. The empirical evidence is that the vitality of religious firms can fluctuate greatly over time, rising as well as falling, although subjective religiousness seems to vary far less.

The interface between secularisation and anti-secularisation arguments tends to relate to areas where the problem is one of differing interpretations of data. Stark and Iannacone, for example, advert to:

> the growing awareness that claims about the progress of secularisation, especially in modern Europe, rest on utterly false perceptions of the widespread piety of these societies in earlier times, and go on to quote Clifford Geertz as saying;

> the anthropological study of religious non-commitment is non-existent. The anthropology of religion will have come of age when some more subtle Malonowski writes a book called Belief and Unbelief (or even Faith and Hypocrisy) in a Savage Society. (Stark and Iannacone, 1994, p.249)

The problem here might be dubbed "the question of the Golden Age"; was there a time when the medieval peasants in their masses were devout and pious Christians? Or is Greeley correct:

> There is no reason to believe that the peasant masses of Europe were ever very devout Christians, not in the sense that we mean when we use these words. There could be no deChristianisation as the term is normally used because there was never any Christianisation in the first place. Christian Europe never existed (ibid. p.241.).

Or again we might ask; was there a golden age of Victorian piety in England to be contrasted with low religious practice in the nineteen nineties? If, like the American sociologist, Talcott Parsons, one measures religiosity by a "bodies on seats" approach, using 1851 census data, then religiosity has indeed declined sharply. If on the other hand one does not employ such "hard" measures, but instead pays attention to the numerous polls and surveys in which the vast majority of respondents affirm belief in God, belief in an afterlife, belief in divinely sanctioned moral imperatives, then perhaps decline in church membership is not evidence of a decline in belief in religious views. In relation to this last controversy Steve Bruce comments:

> I do not accept the anti-secularisation argument that declining participation in organised religion cannot be taken as a decline in belief in the supernatural. Although it is the case that very many non-church members claim some sort of religious experience, when probed on what they have in mind when they make such claims, their answers range from a vague sense that there is more to life than meets the eye, to stories of surviving car crashes which might have been expected to be fatal. (S. Bruce, 1989, p.231)

The question of "a golden age of religious practice", whether it be medieval peasant piety or Victorian church attendance that is viewed in retrospect is an example of a point at which theory is in ferment. Perhaps the scientific paradigm is going to undergo radical readjustment in this particular area of social science. Researchers commenting on a body of obtained data are surely advised to keep in constant dialogue with their findings and in the process of this dialectic to consider how various theoretical perspectives may serve as explanatory tools. For the most part the research project leaned fairly heavily on a Weberian base but at the same time was able to draw on contemporary French sociological thought. Also, within the theoretical framework being used the data threw up unpredicted surprises. It came as a surprise for example to find that the children of classical Pentecostals were the least "sanctified" in terms of devout evangelical piety. Evangelicals generally share a doctrine of Christian initiation which would view it as a unitary process exhibiting a number of facets - repentance of sin, the exercise of faith in Christ as redeemer, reception of the Holy Spirit, and public confession of faith, in the spirit of Romans 10:9 NIV:

> if you confess with your mouth "Jesus is Lord", and believe in your heart that God has raised him from the dead, you will be saved.

Classical Pentecostalism however added to the above a discrete, additional spiritual experience, that of the "baptism in the Holy Spirit", usually evidenced by glossolalia, speaking in tongues. It was therefore unexpected to find believers with a strong Pneumatological[1] emphasis, that is, a strong doctrine of the Holy Spirit, less practically pious in terms of Bible study etc than, say, Christian Brethren pupils. Brethren would generally hold that enthusiastic demonstrations of the Spirit's presence ceased with the completion of the New

Testament canon, that is when the scriptures generally regarded as supremely authoritative had secured the acceptance of the worldwide church. (The book of Revelation was
the last to command general ecumenical acceptance). This view would turn on a particular interpretation of 1 Corinthians 13:10 AV:

> when that which is perfect is come, that which is in part shall pass away,

equating "perfect" with the closure of the NT canon. The quantitative data also threw up unexpected findings - viz that in some respects neither evangelical nor mainline pupils conformed to stereotypical expectations.

Another unexpected finding came from research based on reading newspapers in Alberta, Saskatchewan and Montana, from conversations, and watching television documentaries to the effect that the world rejecting and communitarian Hutterites were thoroughly unpopular with their farmer and rancher neighbours. Paradoxically this dislike is related not so much to attitudinal factors; adherents of the United Reformed Church might, for example, feel that the Hutterites are sitting in judgement on their way of life, a point made strongly in the film "The Perfect Witness", but rather hard economics. Hutterite communal farms become so prosperous that they can buy in bulk from wholesale suppliers in the major cities such as Chicago, and cut out the intervening middlemen in, say, Medicine Hat or Bute. Thus communities of sectaries who eschew capitalist modes of life in their agrarian communes display an ability to work the capitalist system to their best monetary advantage. This came as a surprise because the Hutterite interpretation of Christianity is one that is suffused by the New Testament. Their history also since the days of Jacob Hutter (died 1536), their founder, has generally been characterised by patterns of persecution and subsequent flight; from Germany to Austria, from Austria to Russia, from Russia to the USA, from the USA to Canada (in 1918, because they were reclusive, German speaking and would not join the United States forces). In one sense they are very spiritual, in the New Testament sense of the Greek word pneumatik¢os pneumatikos and had certainly until recently been regarded as helpful neighbours, if somewhat solitary; and yet they operate in such a capitalist fashion as to cut out middle-men - a situation which resonates to our suburban hypermarkets' destruction of town centre small shops.

This is surely a finding which is illuminated primarily by Weberian theory, although one can imagine a classical Marxist drawing attention to the "hard" economics of it. Another paradoxical and unexpected outcome of research into Hutterite communities is to discover that there is a slippage of adherents to conventional American Evangelical churches. It is a commonplace in the sociology of sectarianism that two or three generations on children and grandchildren may begin to move out into the main denominations - but with

Hutterite or Amish "converts" to Billy Graham type crusades and a leaving of the strict, communitarian ethic of the sect, they may in fact, economically speaking, be pursuing "the American dream". Such interviewees on television documentaries may articulate their departure from the sect as "deliverance from bondage", appealing to the text:

Where the spirit of the Lord is, there is liberty. (2 Corinthians 3:17 AV)

Against the anti-secularisation argument, Owen Chadwick, in the Pelican History of the Church series, addressing the topic of the Reformation, in the book "The Reformation" (1964), points out that in discussing its causes, such as the growth of nationalist sentiment, or the new learning, or the discovery of America, one can rule out irreligion. (p.24) He argues that Europe was never more religious, in terms of pilgrimages, penances, the sale of relics, etc., than at that particular period. Indeed, what provoked Luther to nail his 95 Theses on the church door at Wittenberg on All Saint's Day, 1517 had been the preaching of the dominican Monk Tetzel, as he sold indulgences:

As soon as the coin in the coffer rings,
The soul from Purgatory springs.

And also:

Will you then for a mere quarter of a florin receive these letters of indulgence through which you are able to lead a divine and immortal soul into the fatherland of paradise?

Luther remarked ominously, on being apprised of Tetzel's sales:

I'll knock a hole in his drum. (J. Atkinson, 1968, pp.41,42.)

Against this background it is hard to gainsay Weber's argument that the burghers of Calvinistic cities such as Geneva were vulnerable to and influenced by the rationalism associated with the spread of scientific knowledge and the economic changes involved in the decline of feudalism and the transition to capitalism, and became the sober, sturdy, pious entrepreneurs of Switzerland, Holland, New England and elsewhere. The potency of the new ideology they embraced is perhaps illustrated by the contrast between their way of life and spiritual modalities and the practices of the pre-Reformation prince - bishops and rich abbots. The extent to which the changing ideology can be related to the socio-economic base, in straightforward terms, according to a simple base-superstructure pattern, or whether there is involved a dialectic process between base and ideational superstructure, is a nice, subtle problem which has engaged the attention of Marxists and Weberians. Whatever side one is attracted to in that particular debate surely Bryan Wilson is correct to point out that eventually transformations of society which were originally driven by religious ideas come to be self-justificatory in non-religious terms:

> Initially, men sought personal reassurance of their worth in the eyes of God by their worldly success. In the course of a very few decades, capitalism had acquired its own rationale, and achievement had become its own end, without further thought of what it intimated about the divine will. What, under Puritanism, had been a stimulus to action that Weber described as substantively rational, in that it was action that had a given arbitrary end (the glory of God), became, under capitalism, action of a formally rational kind, in which every end was merely the means to some less proximate end. The process was, of course, a religiously inspired transformation of culture. (B. Wilson, 1982, p.77.)

What fascinates about Evangelicals is that they cherish an ideological structure which is essentially not dissimilar to that held by the great Reformers, the Puritan divines or the Wesleyans. To be sure the rigours of Calvinism abated in the face of the more relaxed Arminianism, and in Evangelical thought as a totality many crosscurrents developed. Nor must one forget the third great wing of the Reformation - the Anabaptists or Re-baptisers. One must also remember that pluralism is a tender plant and did not emerge easily - in the sixteenth century the belief "cuius regio, eius religio" "of whom the region, of him the religion" was strongly held; if the king was Anglican then, naturally, the nation was Anglican. Such a conviction was rooted in the notion originally Constantinian, of a church co-terminous with Empire.

As the Reformation gathered pace, the Constantinian unity became fragmented to the extent that a prince who supported Martin Luther might expect his principality, (of which there were a number in the Holy Roman Empire) to become Lutheran religiously. The Anabaptists encountered the same kind of hostility as experienced by say, Jehovah's Witnesses in, say, Italy or Spain, until recent times. Even today, lintels of doors in Malta carry small firmly worded notices warning off sectarian visitors. It was considered to be condign punishment for an Anabaptist leader such as Felix Manz to be roped to a hurdle and thrown into the river to drown, a fate appropriate to a "dipper". This happened in the reformed canton of Zwingli's Zurich. Notoriously, also, Servetus was burnt at the stake in Calvin's Geneva for trinitarian irregularities. In general terms the Anabaptists refused to take up the sword, although one section of them seized the city of Münster and turned it into a violent theocracy. Their lineal descendants such as the Mennonites tended to escape persecution by moving east or west and finishing up in the Americas. It is now generally recognised both by scholars in the mainline churches and by secular historians and sociologists that "the stepchildren of the Reformation" as they came to be known, constituted a major third force within Christianity at large and Evangelicalism in particular. Commenting on the history of the exposition of the Sermon on the Mount the Lutheran theologian Günther Bornkamm says:

> In following this history we find ourselves faced with the question whether the times when the Sermon on the Mount has had special historical significance were not always those in which men allowed themselves to be challenged by Jesus' demand and commandment in a radical and direct fashion and sought, with the most thorough-going personal decision, to put the Sermon on the Mount into practice, quite literally, in their own day, in their refusal to take an oath, by their renunciation of personal property, their "no" to military service. Were not these the truly historical moments, in which the attack upon this world was actually launched and in which the crumbling foundations of its supposedly sacred political, social, moral and religious traditions were shaken; where the volcano of the Sermon on the Mount erupted, or at least where its menacing glow of fire became visible, whose light revealed the precarious lodge upon which Christianity had settled down to a comfortable existence, and upon which it unconcernedly let the flocks of its faithful graze? (Bornkamm, 1960, p.222.)

Bornkamm is clearly thinking here of such things as the Quaker refusal to take up arms or the practice of "affirming" in court, whether the Hutterite practice of "shunning" a recalcitrant brother would command his approval is another matter. One of the "exemplar" interviewees is old enough to have been required to do "National Service", which obtained in Great Britain until the late fifties, and had, upon refusal to serve, as a conscientious objector, been assigned to mining work. Technically the term Anabaptist no longer has meaning, those adherents of churches who apply for baptism as adults are implicitly, or explicitly, repudiating what happened to them as infants, so the prefix ana-, equivalent to re- as an English prefix, is superfluous. In those Evangelical churches which are the spiritual, if not lineal descendants of the Anabaptists, such as the classical Pentecostals, the various kinds of Baptist, Christian Brethren and Evangelical Independents the usual practice followed is for older children and adolescents to apply for baptism, upon or after conversion, and the imagery of Romans 6:4 AV:

> Therefore we are buried with Him by baptism into death: that like as Christ was raised up from the dead by the glory of the Father, even so we also should walk in newness of life,

would serve as justification for the mode of immersion, rather than, say, affusion.

Such is the rich tapestry of Evangelicalism, spreading from the radical Hutterites across the denominations to Roman Catholic charismatics. It has already been shown how the Evangelical world has its own internal structures

128

and networks. The majority of the pupils and students interviewed as Evangelicals would have been members of or attached to their school or church Scripture Union (or Christian Union in Universities and Colleges). This factor indeed was a very important one for our research assistant as she went about recruiting a sample. Those who deemed themselves Evangelical but abjured any contact with school Scripture Unions or Christian Unions would have done so on the grounds of separation - they might have had conscientious reservations about the ecumenical movement and have not wished to sit under the ministry of clergy whose churches were affiliated to the World Council of Churches, or if adherents of glossolalist churches may have felt themselves uncomfortable in the presence of fellow Evangelical pupils who were adherents on non-enthusiastic groups.

Nor is it only as a contemporaneous or synchronic phenomenon that Evangelicalism presents itself as a variegated tapestry. Historically too, or diachronically it is possible to view it as in one sense a unitary phenomenon but in another as one which subsumes into itself many diversities. Perhaps one finds, as does Bebbington, the "lift-off" of modern English and American Evangelicalism in Wesley's time, or perhaps one feels that the continuities running back to the Puritans and the Reformers are too strong for such a hypothesis, or perhaps the Anabaptist wing of the Reformation has not been paid enough attention. As previously noted, E. H. Broadbent in "The Pilgrim Church" (1931) advanced an evangelical Anabaptist-type theory to the effect that a sacred thread of what he regarded as truly scriptural practice ran right back through history to the apostolic churches, back beyond the Lollards and Huss and their followers through the Waldensian and Albigensians, the Paulicians and the Nestorians to the first century sources. This claim is not dissimilar to the "high" Calvinism which would see the presbyterates of the Protestant cantons as standing in a lineal relationship to those generations of presbyters who had passed on the apostolic faith - the need being, as Calvin saw it, to revive those ecclesiastical practices only which came from the time "ante papatum"; "before the papacy", as he put it. But Broadbent's claim of an agelong witness would be cast in a much more exclusive register and he would have regarded Calvin as having been only partially enlightened.

It is not however simply a matter of historical/theological diversities - that Wesley for example, was of Arminian convictions whereas his great "deputy" Whitefield was a Calvinist or that Luther argued for a doctrine of consubstantiation - viz. that the body and blood of Christ were present in an non-local sense "in, with and under" the bread and wine, (Atkinson, 1968, p.60.), whereas Zwingli viewed the communion as a commemorative act, a seal of what the believer was already well aware of on the grounds of the gospel (Atkinson, p.100.). Nor is it only a matter of historical diversities. Social movement theorists draw our attention to the fact that:

the argument can be made that British and American evangelicalism were both denominationally and class diverse throughout the nineteenth century. The evangelical revival that swept across England in the late eighteenth and early nineteenth centuries broke out among three distinct religious groups: the working-class and the lower middle-class followers at Wesley, the skilled working-class and middle-class members of older dissenting churches (i.e. Baptist, Presbyterian and Congregational) and upper-class members of the church of England. ...... evangelicalism was itself an avenue for upward social mobility for the working-class poor. (J. C. Soper, 1994, p.45.)

Soper goes on to note that:

British evangelicals are *not* predominantly working-class. (p.48)

This last insight chimes in with our research experience. The schools in which we located our sixth form sample were mainly voluntary, selective grammars and the middle-class background of pupils was everywhere apparent, with few exceptions. This applied to both elements of the research cohort, evangelical and Mainline. And when it came to discussing possible senior figures to approach for interview we were confronted with a wealth of possibilities ranging from millionaire businessmen to medical consultants of world stature. The worldwide reputation of the Ulster universities, schools and hospitals is such that foreign students and visiting academics, particularly from the Far and Middle East flock there. Many of these are Evangelical Christians. Soper (1994) notes that the class profile for Evangelicals in North America is one in which liberal Protestants are significantly more highly represented amongst those who complete higher education courses but that this picture is changing in favour of Evangelicals.

Given the diversely rich texture of Evangelicalism across the world what general characteristics may one posit of the movement? Firstly, Evangelicals are comfortable with modernity. Steve Bruce comments:

.... conservative Protestantism 'fits' with the modern world. At the most abstract level of cognitive style one finds a basic resonance between the ways of thinking about the world that are common to conservative Protestants, and the rational and empiricist epistemology of a Baconian natural science. While the belief system of the conservative Protestant contains propositions about a supernatural realm, the style of reasoning is similar to the rationalism of the secular world. Thus, provided the believer can neutralise actual propositions that conflict with his beliefs, he can continue to work within a scientific world view, as the large number of English evangelicals to be found in medicine and natural science demonstrates. (S. Bruce, 1984, p.204.)

Our Evangelical interviewees are nicely described by the Latin phrase "homines unius libri", "people of one book", and Barr (1978) argues that in contemporary Evangelicalism the inerrancy of scripture is the lynchpin doctrine so "the Word" assumes a pivotal centrality. In terms of an epistemology, a doctrine of knowledge, such a biblicist perspective leads to a view of knowledge as an objectively given "out-there" datum. The inspired word of scripture is regarded as the fount of truth and as a kind of static standard against which to evaluate all matters of faith and morals, and indeed in the more conservative circles, matters such as geology and biology. In our interviews there was encountered a certain Puritan bluntness, particularly with the surgeon and the vet, which resonates with the epistemological "black and white-ness". Surgeons and vets of course are notoriously busy people and it may be that there is an interplay between the demands of a busy professional life and an externally conceived ethic. Bluntness and directness, as Puritan characteristics, do not amount to brusqueness; the surgeon was particularly concerned about the quality of personal relationships with fellow professionals such as nurses, and with doing the utmost for one's patients. In the current atmosphere of late capitalism, where aggressive and "macho" styles of management are overtly encouraged a research effort might profitably examine the extent to which Evangelical managers reconcile the tension between the demands imposed by the profit motive and the scriptural exhortations to masters about humane treatment of slaves.

Historically, Quaker employers such as the Rowntrees and the Cadburys resolved the kind of ideological tension between the demands of a capitalist ethic and the New Testament moral imperatives to do everything "as to the Lord and not to men" (Ephesians 6:7 AV) by a benign paternalism towards their workforces. More recently the Christian Brethren businessman Sir John Laing endowed the Laing Trust with many millions of pounds as a kind of beneficent reserve on which various Evangelical groupings might draw. The Laing company was also characterised by a certain twentieth-century type paternalism towards its workers and executives, particularly those of longstanding experience in the service of the firm. It is difficult to gauge the extent to which, dispassionately viewed, paternalism of the Quaker type might be construed as ultimately injurious to the growth of truly pluralist democracy, because in their chronological and socio-cultural context workers' villages, or schools for workers' children, were often innovations. Similarly it is difficult when considering the Laing fund or similar Evangelical financial repositories which have built hospitals and schools in the third world not to bear in mind the negative evaluations of some sociologists. John Gunstone, a high Anglican charismatic apologist comments in this connection:

> Itinerant preachers like Finney, Moody and Torrey depended for at least part of their lives on the support of wealthy businessmen. Some of those

who made fortunes through the expansion of agriculture, commerce and industry financed the evangelists' campaigns, even building special halls in cities for their rallies. Although these evangelists and their benefactors did not lack social concern and their charitable works were many, this support from the wealthy linked the revivalist-holiness tradition with political conservatism.

Sociologists have suggested that an unconscious motive for supporting the evangelists and the movements they represented was an attempt by the upper and middle classes to neutralise the threat of an emerging and powerful working-class in Western society.

Bringing the matter up to date Gunstone continues:

This political colouring is still evident in bodies which have promoted the charismatic renewal in America, such as the Full Gospel Business Men's Fellowship International, American charismatics are sometimes shocked to find so many English charismatics leaning towards the other side of the political spectrum. (Gunstone, 1982, pp.59,60.)

The sorts of moral and political conundrums which can be taken up by the intermingling of a New Testament ethic with developing or late capitalism are sometimes alleviated for conservative christians by the conviction that their citizenship, in an ultimate sense, lies in heaven, (Philippians 3:20 NIV) and that they are pilgrims passing through this present world. If it happens to be a late capitalist world then one is called on to live in it and work within it, always keeping in mind that one's spiritual centre of gravity, essentially, lies elsewhere, in the Beyond. Thus life is lived out in a tension between a this-worldly scenario, which may involve the riches of a Carnegie, or (if one be a Chinese Christian) a vale of tears, and a world-beyond modality, as in Hebrews 12:22 NIV:

But you have come to Mount Zion, to the heavenly Jerusalem, the city of the Living God.

Of course, if one is conscious of the demands upon one, morally speaking, emanating from a supernal realm, and mediated by scripture, and if one's cognitive style is constrained by an epistemology which very much perceives "the Beyond" as a supernaturalist projection, "out-there" then one is going to exemplify the Calvinist-type virtues. Black is black and white is white and little weight, if any, will be accorded to insights about subjective or social considerations in the construction of knowledge. But it is not simply a matter of a particular scientific mode of thinking. Christopher Hill comments:

Puritanism aided science by its abolition of mystery, its emphasis on law, its insistence on direct, personal relationship to God and co-operation with

132

him. (Hill, 1970, p.229)

Externally this Protestant individualism involved the substantial reduction of a complicated sacramental system. The seven sacraments of the Roman church, baptism, the eucharist, penance, unction, orders, marriage, confirmation functioned as channels through which the medicine of heavenly grace could be poured into the hearts and lives of believers. But the secularising tendency of Protestantism reduced the seven to two or none, in the sense that the bread and wine were regarded as symbolic elements, as with most of the Anabaptists, or were spiritualised out of existence as with the Quakers. The overall effect of this reductionism was to emphasise the individual and the subjective as over against the corporate and objective. The mediaeval Catholic teaching of "ex opere operato" (Latin - as a result of the deed having been carried out) taught that the sacrament of the mass, when the liturgy was duly performed by a properly ordained priest acted on the believer like a fire in winter acts upon a freezing man - he/she merely has to be there to receive its warmth - in the Catholic interpretation, even if there happened to be the rarity of an evilly inclined man officiating, the sacrament, by virtue of the objective nature of its operation, still exerted an influence for good on the soul, the only barrier being internal hostile dispositions of the heart and behind the administration of each sacrament stood the majestic collective authority of the church. In differing degrees the varying Protestant emphases watered down these objectivities. For example, the Anglican theologian Hooker was to say of the eucharist:

the real presence of Christ's most blessed body and blood is not to be sought for in the Sacrament but in the worthy receiver of the Sacrament. (Atkinson, 1968, p.259.)

In the theological terminology of the time such words would have been described as exemplifying a virtualist and receptionist view of the sacrament, i.e. that sacramental efficacy is dependent on the subjective state of heart before God of the receiver of it. From a sociological or anthropological viewpoint they can be seen as a subjectivising of it or a demystifying of the magic. Protestantism was essentially a faith for the individual who had a subjective relationship with God. The concept of priesthood came to be understood symbolically and metaphorically as in the words of 1 Peter 2:5 AV:

Ye also, as lively stones, are built up a spiritual house, an holy priesthood, to offer up spiritual sacrifices, acceptable to God by Jesus Christ,

and 1 Peter 2:9 AV:

But yea are a chosen generation, a royal priesthood, an holy nation, a peculiar people.

It was not now a matter of any objectively defined sacerdotal caste working on one's behalf and being validated ex-officio (by virtue of the office) but of individuals relating to God for salvation and reassurance as individuals and for whom the sacerdotalism of tabernacle and temple in the Old Testament functioned solely as types and shadows. As Paul says in 1 Corinthians 10:11AV:

> Now all these things happened unto them for ensamples: and they are written for our admonition upon whom the ends of the world are come.

From the Lutheran/Calvinist point of view the simple message of the New Testament - salvation through faith in Christ had been heavily overlaid by the mediaeval re-introduction of a complex sacredotal and sacramental system; there was a need for a return to the simple old-fashioned verities. Steve Bruce comments:

> Unlike its major competitors, Protestantism is a faith for the individual. Nations and societies are not saved; only individual repentant sinners can attain salvation. The primacy of the individual allows Protestantism to adapt to the shift from the public and the social to the private and the familial that one finds in modern societies. (S. Bruce, 1984, p.20)

Certainly the stress on the individual and on the private relationship with God characterise our research findings. The concept of the "quiet time" even though not designated as such, is deeply rooted in the Evangelical psyche. The desideratum is an early morning "slot" of 15 minutes to an hour devoted to prayer and bible-reading. Devotional aids of the "Every Day with Jesus" type or the Scripture Union notes format are cast into a kind of gobbett mode, i.e. a psalm, or a paragraph of scripture for meditation, with accompanying notes of an explanatory or devotional nature. Such an approach to bible study perhaps serves to forment atomistic perceptions - scripture comes to be perceived as a collectivity of individual verses. This individualistic religious exercise is particularly characteristic of conservative Protestantism. As Steve Bruce remarks:

> but of the two main varieties, it is the conservative form that most easily fits new concerns. Liberal Protestantism has a tendency to focus on the social rather than personal. This can be seen in the tendency to left-wing politics and in the notion of relevance. (S.Bruce, ibid. 1984, p.205)

Bruce perhaps has in mind here the fact that in the sixties and seventies the Student Christian Movement became so radicalised that its energies were dissipated into a number of extreme left directions until it had to be disbanded, a comment perhaps on the accelerated secularisation associated with the demythologisation of the Bible and creeds. But Bruce is surely correct about Evangelicalism and the focus on the personal and the individual, a factor so important in our differentiated, industrialised, urbanised society where the ethos is one of Gesellschaft at the macro-level rather than of Gemeinschaft, of means to end type communities (dormitory suburbs) rather than ends-in-themselves communal entities (community schools integrated into communities). Along with an emphasis on the personal and the individual, Protestantism also brought with it a penchant for independence of thought, rooted in regular Bible reading. As Christopher Hill remarks:

> The protestant doctrine of the priesthood of all believers opened doors to innovation, because it was ultimately an appeal to individual interpretation of the Bible, to the consciences of (some) individual laymen and women. (Hill, 1993, p.416.)

The sturdy individualism so encouraged by such practices as individual Bible-study manifested itself in other ways. By the time the Reforming movement had "bedded down" so to speak there was a spectrum of churchmanship running from Lutheranism, which was essentially a reformed Catholicism, right over to independency, Quakerism and Anabaptism. The ideal of a congregationalist polity is individualism writ large. Each gathered church is responsible through its eldership to God alone and is independent of its sister churches administratively. It is, in this vision of ecclesiastical autonomy, as if "the church which is His body" (Ephesians 1:23 AV) is like some subterranean rock formation which in various places pokes up through the soil in rocky outcrops. In this analogy, each outcrop functions as an autonomous unit of the church. It is not surprising that Weber was particularly struck by the business acumen and success of people of this temper, particularly Quakers and Mennonites. Contemporaneously many churches of Evangelical and Congregational polity are affiliated to FIEC, the Fellowship of Independent Evangelical Churches, and many groupings would be found under the general title of Christian Brethren. It is difficult to find statistics about the latter, given the fact that many congregations disclaim any appellation other than that they are Christians of the locality meeting according to Matt 18:20 AV:

> Where two or three are gathered together in my name, there am I in the midst of them,

but as a known grouping within Evangelical culture the Brethren, as with Weber's Quakers and Mennonites, would be noted for the concentration within their ranks of successful businessmen and of high ranking members of the professions. (This would no longer be true of the Exclusive Brethren, who feel unable to take the "sponsio academica"[2] of university matriculation ceremonies or to be part of university convocations, on the grounds of fellowship with unbelievers). Many of the Christian or Open Brethren would seem to summate in their own personae the Weberian notion of the individualist both in spiritual and commercial/ professional terms. And it is particularly amongst Christian Brethren and similar groups that there is cherished the ideal of congregationalist autonomy - a kind of assembly or ecclesia-type individualism which is believed to replicate the New Testament church polity.

Steve Bruce isolates a further factor which helps Evangelicals to be comfortable with modernity, that of an underlying pessimism.

> Liberalism involves an essentially hopeful and optimistic picture of man and his ability to improve himself and his world. Conservative forms of Protestantism tend to assert the total sinfulness and depravity of man. In a world of nuclear weapons, apparently uncontrollable economies, pollution and terrorism, the notion that man is inherently sinful has considerable appeal. The last decade seems to have been characterised by an increase in general conservatism in the Western world and such a change in political climate adds to the general 'plausibility' of conservative Protestantism. .... The right has been able to capitalise on a loss of faith in government and the increase in popularity of right wing individualism again aids conservative Protestantism. (S. Bruce, 1984, p.205.)

The comment needs to be made here that there is a very real ideational gap between liberal and conservative Protestantism. The pessimism of fundamentalist type Evangelicalism is rooted in an inerrant doctrine of scriptural inspiration which does not allow as much room for manoeuvre as is afforded to the liberal. It is not that modern Evangelicals fully share the pessimistic outlook enunciated in "5-point" Calvinism and illustrated by the mnemonic acronym TULIP.

Contentious matters such as these are put into the background. Charles Simeon's dictum would be followed by many 20th century Evangelicals viz, that he was "a Calvinist when praying, and an Arminian when preaching".[3]

Modern Evangelical statements of faith tend to focus on the inerrancy of scripture as originally given, trinitarianism, the universality and reality of sin the substitutionary atonement of Christ, as in the hymn stanza:

> In my place condemned he stood,
> Sealed my pardon with his blood.,

the Resurrection of Jesus from the dead, the convicting and indwelling work of the Holy Spirit, personally conceived of, not as an impersonal or vague influence, and the physical Second Return of Jesus. Some statements would add to the above skeletal outline a rider as to the reality, in some sense, and eternity, of hell but John Stott (1988, p.320) indicates that there is a place in modern Evangelical thinking for annihilationism; the doctrine that the impenitent will perish completely and forever in the Divine judgement. But Evangelicals do not feel free to follow liberals all the way in restating the faith in modern categories.

This is why they hold Calvinist and Arminian insights in a kind of permanent tension, and, as it were, for reasons of Evangelical unity and evangelism, "shelve" them. But if Karl Barth boldly rearranges the theological furniture of predestination doctrine so that all penitent sinners are condemned with Christ, the representative Man, as He absorbs the Wrath of God, and all are risen with Him in Resurrection to new life, Evangelicals will feel bound to measure any such reconstructions by the word of scripture to which they feel themselves anchored. Or if liberal theologians interpret the doctrine of the Second Coming teleologically as meaning that God's creation is moving in a purposive direction Evangelicals will prefer to think of Acts 1:10,11 AV:

> And while they looked steadfastly toward heaven as he went up, behold, two men stood by them in white apparel, which also said, Ye men of Galilee, why stand ye gazing up into heaven? This same Jesus, which is taken up from you into heaven, shall so come in like manner as ye have seen him go into heaven.

The word of scripture is decisive for Evangelicals in such situations, although a famous Evangelical of the last century, Charles Haddon Spurgeon, of the Metropolitan Tabernacle, London, rebuked his fellow-believers at Plymouth with the words:

Ye men of Plymouth, Why stand ye gazing upwards,

a comment on J. N. Darby's eschatological emphasis.

Conservative Evangelicals, particularly as constituted in "gathered churches", or "faith-missions", that is assemblies of believers where all adherents are voluntarist and participant members, and missionary-type enterprises which neither publicise their needs nor canvas for money, will often in a sort of short-hand, refer to Evangelicals past and present as "the Lord's people", or "of the family of Jacob"; a reference to the Genesis patriarch and his familial connections. Despite the claim that modern Evangelicalism begins with great preachers such as Wesley or Jonathan Edwards in the USA, they would look back past them to Richard Baxter, to Ridley and Latimer, Anglican bishops burnt at the stake by "bloody Mary" and further back to the Reformers themselves and behind them the Lollards and the Waldenses, the Bogomils of Bosnia and the Paulicians of Asia Minor, as spiritual progenitors. If questioned, they would attribute the success of Evangelicals to divine blessing. Sociologists profer explanations which do not invoke any supernatural realities. As Steve Bruce puts it:

> The success of conservative Protestantism lies in its ability to resonate with the interests of the secular world while still preserving its own distinct identity. (S. Bruce, 1984, p.206.)

Such a comment would probably elicit from Evangelicals a reference to some scriptural passage such as 1 Corinthians 5:9-11 NIV:

> I have written to you in my letter not to associate with sexually immoral people - not at all meaning the people of this world who are immoral, or the greedy and swindlers, or idolators. In that case you would have to leave this world. But now I am writing to you that you must not associate with anyone who calls himself a brother but is sexually immoral, or greedy, an idolator or a slanderer, a drunkard or a swindler. With such a man do not even eat.

In this passage dealing with internal church discipline Paul makes it clear that the believer is called on to go out into the secular world and mix in day-to-day life. In other passages he extols the virtues of hard work out there in the world and is particularly proud to remind converts how he had plied his trade in order not to be burdensome. As he remarks in 1 Thessalonians 1:9 NIV:

> Surely you remember, brothers, our toil and hardship; we worked night and day in order not to be a burden to any one while we preached the gospel of God to you.

Paul's trade in fact was that of tent-maker (Greek skhnopoL¢os) or leather worker. Evangelicals thus have a solid scriptural fundament for going out into the hurly-burly of the secular world to earn a living, apart from groups which espouse the communitarianism of the primitive church (of Acts Chapter 4). This concept, as previously noted, gained theological articulation in terms of the notion of the calling. In a liberal Protestant comment on vocation John M Barkley says:

> The Church is not a camp of refugees from earthly society. Her members go not into monasteries, but are participants in thousands of vocations, in which they serve, and co-operate with, their fellow-men and not simply their fellow Christians. (Barkley, 1966, p.63.)

Our research has found that without exception Evangelicals are concerned very profoundly about vocation and would, if feeling a definite call to serve in a medical capacity in a mission hospital of the Leprosy Mission in India, set about equipping themselves to obey the divine call and go, whether as teacher, nurse or doctor. The calling to be a missionary doctor seemed to be much in the mind of interviewees and it is tempting to arrive at a negative conclusion, namely, that Evangelical aspirations towards vocations have a utilitarian dimension to them, whereas Mainline aspirations were more vague and less clearcut. But the primacy of medical vocations is perhaps related to the missionary nature of Evangelicalism - in hostile or forbidden countries medical service has historically acted as an "Open Sesame" to evangelistic doors that would otherwise have remained closed.

If, however, the locating of the service of God in the various occupations of everyday life is in itself a secularising process, removing the locus of devotion from the cloister to the marketplace, Evangelicalism has assuredly not gone down the secularising path as far as others. Not for it the neo-orthodoxy of Barth or the demythologising programme of the school of Bultmann, or the radicalism of the Death of God theologians. It has maintained a solid scaffolding of conservative doctrine, not compromising any of the elements of what it regards as the irreducible core of Christian conviction. Thus, for example, ECONI, (the acronym stands for Evangelical Contribution to Northern Ireland) is a group of Evangelicals who are concerned with reconciliation with Roman Catholics, but make the point that they are not "ecumenical" by which they mean that they are not tainted by liberal protestant "dilutions" of the "faith which was once delivered to the saints" Jude 3 AV. As J. C. Soper notes:

> The strictness of Evangelical doctrines has helped them sustain distinct social groups and religious cultures in the past two centuries as the distance between Evangelicals and non-Evangelicals has grown. (Soper, 1994, p.50.)

It is something of a truism in the Western world that conservative churches have been growing whereas liberal churches have been in decline. The retention of ideological purity is concomitant with a refusal to compromise on perceived essentials of doctrine. A degree of latitude is extended to the arcane details of fringe areas of the belief-system, such as the details surrounding end-of-the-world scenarios, provided that belief in the central fact of a Second Coming in some sort of literal sense is retained. Identity therefore seems inextricably bound up with soundness of doctrine but the parameters of "separation from the world" seem susceptible to adjustment. When we were planning this research project we had in mind several stories related to us by teacher colleagues of girls from Evangelical halls who in the seventies and eighties had become head girls of grammar schools. When the annual school formal dance came around four were known to have refused to wear formal ball-gowns or participate in the dance but had received guests in school uniform and helped to cook and serve supper. We later heard of North American valedictorians, the equivalent of head-boy or girl who had acted precisely in the same manner. In the first year of the project however there appeared in the provincial evening paper a picture of the formal dance at a large, local voluntary grammar school, and in the centre of the photo was the head girl, daughter of a medical consultant, clad in full ball gown, - a communicant member of a local Gospel Hall. Perhaps such an account is symptomatic of an Evangelical adjustment of the boundary, from time to time, in matters of social intercourse.

There are of course geographically determined cultural differences. As F. F. Bruce remarks:

An American theologian remarked in my hearing that somebody ought one day to write a PhD thesis on "regional holiness". He had in mind various religions in the United States in whose conception of practical holiness attitudes to (say) tobacco, alcohol, dancing and the theatre play a prominent but varying part, and his point was that the variation in attitudes frequently depended not on denominational connexion but on geographical residence. (Bruce, 1970, p.17.)

Varieties of ecclesiastical membership also may colour social behaviour. The Gospel Hall and Bible Chapels of North America spring from the same historical root, but the former eschew organised summer camps whilst the latter not only organise camps but field local sports teams. The American Assemblies of God require adherents to abjure tobacco and alcohol, but modern charismatics enjoy wine in moderation.

A great strength of groups such as Evangelicals is the voluntarism involved. Members of the movement are members by conviction, whether they have grow up in Evangelical families or churches or are recent converts. They are people who have chosen to live their lives out according to the tenets of that particular world view. The other side of the voluntarist coin however is that everyone knows that if the ideological package begins to be less than satisfactory then it is time to resign, or at least to fade away. Parents are aware that, if they send their children to the School Scripture Union group meeting, or the Children's Seaside Special Mission, the CSSM, they will only hear "sound", i.e. fundamentalist teaching. This may be implicit in certain situations, explicit in others. In the mid-fifties, the SCM at Cambridge invited the then Bishop of Durham, Michael Ramsay, to conduct a mission to the University entitled "The Scandal of the Church". The "CICCU Coll. Reps", i.e. the thirty odd representatives of the colleges decided collectively to dissuade any CICCU members from attending, lest they encounter doubts and difficulties.

Such a conviction about the preservation of theological purity means that Evangelicals can exercise discipline in order to strengthen the body of believers. A "black and white" species of excommunication is not in view, although this can happen in the smaller Evangelical sects. Deviant belief or behaviour however will render one unacceptable to the network and invitations to speak or hold office will dry up, social intercourse will wither away. In this way the congregation purifies and strengthens itself.

The most striking and memorable features of Evangelical beliefs and behaviour, which leave the most lasting impressions are the conviction of the proximity at all times of the divine. This is particularly evident with the exemplar surgeon in his operating theatre or the sixth formers feeling that God would help them as they sat their exams. Equally striking is the love of the Bible and the obedience to its teaching as evidenced by the numerous accounts of daily bible-study and

140

of learning Greek and about Hebrew. There is also the vocational willingness to serve God wherever in the world the call might be, accompanied by a serious attitude to life and the absence of any frivolous concern and the industry and ambition to do well.

Interviewees were obviously committed to a path in life which was going to eventuate in both a very Protestant type of spirituality and worldly success, whether in terms of professional distinction or business acumen. In terms of their beliefs they would probably contest the notion of being driven by a fear of being predestined to hell, a doctrine which has been effectively shelved by Evangelicalism. They were not in the same circumstances as those whom Giddens describes as having been driven by such a belief, or as suffering from "salvation panic" by Christopher Hill. To an extent, even though Evangelicalism has retained a residual core of "correct" doctrine it has inevitably been influenced by liberal Protestantism. The worldview of the sixteenth century had a secure place within it for a literal hell of burning coals and an eternity of suffering and Evangelicals still affirm the reality of eternal punishment in some sense but it tends to be rather a C. S. Lewis version out of the Screwtape Letters, a sort of gloomy eternal separation from the Divine presence. Such a conviction is more tolerable of belief in the twentieth century.

Conclusion

Bryan Wilson comments:

> At present, in the West, the remnants of religion are, if receding, as yet still in evidence, but generally it may be said that western culture lives off the borrowed capital of its religious past. It is by no means clear what sort of society is coming into being as religious values wane. The consequences, not only for the arts and high culture, but also, and perhaps more importantly, for the standards of civic order, social responsibility, and individual integrity, may be such that the future of western civilisation itself may be thrown into jeopardy. To opine that these effects might ensue, is not, of course, to imply that the particular religious values of western society were in any sense either intrinsically warranted or specifically necessary for the maintenance of civilised order. It is, rather, to suggest that at least in the functions that were in the past supplied by, or at least supported by, religion, may now be left unserviced, and so to raise the question of whether in the future the conditions of life will ever be wholly humane without the operation of some such agencies. (Wilson, 1982, p.88.)

To this somewhat pessimistic evaluation is added a further comment:

As everyday life in modern society demands ever extending commitment to rational procedures, so the personal, religiously-inspired caveats of the truly religious man are likely to become increasingly vestigial, and he the more likely to acquire a sense of his own marginality. (p.175.)

To say that "western culture lives off the borrowed capital of its religious past" is to admit that under the conditions of modernity obtaining in late 20th century capitalism, the old perceived moral warmth of a more paternalistic society is replaced by rational and technical considerations. Approaching the beginning of the third millennium of our era we are non-plussed by the intractable nature of the problems posed by late capitalism. In the most sophisticated modern economies impersonal forces appear to create macro-structural unemployment. The concept of a unilinear career-pattern is eroded in favour of a constant re-training and re-adaptation to new circumstances. Computerisation, hastened on by micro-chip technologies, scythes through professions and industries throwing thousands out of work. Just as early incipient capitalism deskilled multitudes by making them cogs in mass production processes so late capitalism foments the forces of dehumanisation by lionising the profit motive and the operation of market forces. One contemporary Evangelical voice, that of Martyn Eden comments about our social predicament:

We will cite the current divorce rates, the number of one-parent families, the growing incidence of illegitimacy and rape, the number of abortions, the evidence of alcohol and drug abuse, and the neglect of old people, and we will call for the recovery of biblical values regarding the family and sexual morality. (Eden, 1991, p.171.)

This statement might be characterised as an appeal for a return to community values derived from and supported by religious, super-empirical intimations as a way of solving contemporary social and moral problems. It prompts the question as to what contribution Evangelicals have made to the centuries-old debate about the consequences of moving from familiar and interwoven communities to large impersonal societies. What have Evangelicals said in the past? What do contemporary Evangelicals have to say to us about our current dilemmas?

In the past the Evangelicals have constituted a powerful critique in the socio-political context of its time, as when the sustained campaign of Wilberforce against slavery bore fruit in its abolition. But at other times, the voice of critique and protest has been muted and they have appeared to have been in pietistic retreat. Many are aware of this, as is evidenced by the books, "The Contemporary Christian" by John Stott (IVP, 1992) and "The Gospel in the Modern World" edited by M. Eden and D. F. Wells (IVP, 1991) and in parts of these books a revived social awareness is encouraged and critiques are advanced of varieties of socialism and capitalism. Addressing, however, a specific American audience Steve Bruce comments:

> The American conservative Protestant tradition displays frequent alternation between periods of active involvement and retreat. Even when the activist element has been dominant there have been those who decry social and political involvement as a diversion, a waste of the energy which should be directed to the primary task of saving souls. (1988, p.175.)

It may be that there is built into the Evangelical psyche as a whole some kind of oscillation between activism and quietism such as Bruce here attributes to American Evangelicals. There are parallels here perhaps with other groups. Within Roman Catholicism the advocates of "liberation theology" are wont to discuss " unjust political structures" and the pros and cons of "armed struggle", but in so doing appear to earn the disapprobation of Pope John Paul II, who urges upon such activists the value of prayer, and who looks back on a lifetime of co-existing with a communist political order. Or, within an Anglican context, when the African provinces and bishops are about to legitimise the concept of armed struggle as a result of their political critique, an impassioned rebuttal is delivered by Archbishop Robin Eames of the Church of Ireland against the background of the Irish troubles.

The main factor involved is one of religious vision. The conservative Evangelical discourse is one which always retains within its purview the nearness and seriousness of eternal matters and of the presence in this world of the eternal in terms of a physically conceived eschatology. Against this background the urgency of political critiques of phases such as empire, mercantilism and free trade are adjudged to be less clamant than that of evangelisation of the world.

Notes

1. In NT Greek the word for "spirit" is "pneüma", i.e. transliterated "pneuma".
2. The "sponsio academica" was a kind of student Hippocratic oath, taken at the outset of a university course. Such formal matriculation ceremonies are no longer commonly held, but in the sixties this constituted a burning issue for groups such as exclusives.
3. Charles Simeon left such an impression on the collective Cambridge mind that even as late as the 1950's the term "sim" was used as a kind of equivalent to "bible-thumper".

Bibliography

Atkinson, J. (1968), *The Great Light*, Paternoster, London.

Barkley, J.M. (1966), *Presbyterianism*, Steele, Belfast.

Barr, J. (1973), *The Bible in the Modern World*, Student Christian Movement, London.

Barr, J. (1977), *Fundamentalism*, Student Christian Movement, London.

Barr, J. (1984), *Escaping from Fundamentalism*, Student Christian Movement, London.

Barth, K. (1927), *Dogmatik I*, Vorwort, Muenchen.

Barth, K. (1957), *Church Dogmatics II The Doctrine of God Part 2*, T. and T. Clark, Edinburgh, 1957 English Translation of 1948.

Barth, K. (1958), *The Faith of the Church*, Meridian.

Bebbington, D.W. (1989), *Evangelicalism in Modern Britain*, Unwin Hyman, London.

Beer, P. (1968), *Mrs Beer's House*, Anthony Mott Ltd., London.

Berger, P. & Luckman, T. (1967), *The Social Construction of Reality*, Penguin, London.

Berger, P.L. (1969), *The Social Reality of Religion*, Faber, London.

Bornkamm, G. (1973), *Jesus of Nazareth*, Hodder and Stoughton, London.

Bourdieu, P. (1971), 'Intellectual Field and Creative Project' in Young M.F.D. ed. *Knowledge and Control*, Collier MacMillan, London.

Bourdieu, P. (1990), *In Other Words*, Polity Press, Cambridge.

Bridger, F. (1988), *Children Finding Faith*, Scripture Union, London.

Broadbent, E.H. (1931), *The Pilgrim Church*, Pickering and Inglis, London and Glasgow.

Bronowski, J. (1976), *The Ascent of Man*, BBC, London.

Bruce, F.F. (1950), *The Books and the Parchments*, Pickering and Inglis, London.

Bruce, F.F. (1951), *The Acts of the Apostles*, The Tyndale Press, London.

Bruce, F.F. (1958), *The Spreading Flame*, Paternoster, London.

Bruce, F.F. (1963), *The Epistle of Paul to the Romans*, The Tyndale Press, London.

Bruce, F.F. (1970), *Tradition Old and New,* Paternoster, London.

Bruce, F.F. (1972), *Answers to Questions*, Paternoster, London.

Bruce, S. (1984), *Firm in the Faith*, Gower, Aldershot.

Bruce, S. (1986), *God Save Ulster*, Oxford University Press, Oxford.

Bruce, S. (1988),*The Rise and Fall of the New Christian Right,* Clarendon Press, Cambridge.

Bruce, S. (1994), *The Edge of the Union*, Oxford University Press, Oxford.

Cicourel (1973), *Cognitive Sociology*, Penguin, London.

Chadwick, O. (1964), *The Reformation*, Penguin, London.

Child, D. (1970), *The Essentials of Factor Analysis*, Holt, Rhinehart & Nelson, London.

Cicourel (1973), *Cognitive Sociology,* Penguin, London.

Coad, F. Roy (1968), *A History of the Brethren Movement*, Paternoster Press, Exeter, England.

Cohen, L. & Manion, L. (1989), *Research Methods in Education,* , Routledge, Kegan and Paul, London.

Davidson, J. C. & Caddell, D.C. (1994), 'Religion and the Meaning of Work', *Journal for the Scientific Study of Religion*, June, Vol.33, No.2, pp.135-147.

Davies, H. (1954), *Christian Deviations*, Student Christian Movement, London.

Echoes Missionary Magazine, Echoes of Service, Bath, June 1994.

Eden, M. & Wells, D.F. (eds.), (1991), *The Gospel in the Modern World*, Inter-Varsity Press, Leicester.

Edwards, D.L. and Stott, J.(1988), *Essentials: A Liberal-Evangelical Dialogue*, Hodder and Stoughton, London.

Foster, Roger (1986), *Ten New Churches*, Marc Europe, The British Church Growth Association, Harrow.

Giddens, A. (1985), 'Introduction', in Weber, M., *The Protestant Ethic and the Spirit of Capitalism*, Counterpoint, London.

Gorman, E. A. (1994), *From a Log Cabin in 1908 - A History of the Highway Gospel Hall*, Kelowna Copy Centre, Canada.

Glaser, B. & Straus, A. (1967), *The Discovery of Grounded Theory*, Weidenfield & Nicholson, London.

Gosse, E. (1907), *Father and Son.*, Heinemann, London.

Gunstone, J. (1982), *Pentecostal Anglicans.* Hodder & Stoughton, London.

Hadden, J. K. (1993), 'Review of Stark and Bainbridge (1987), "A Theory of Religion", Lang, New York', *Journal for the Scientific Study of Religion*, December, Vol.32, No.4, pp.402,403.

Hammmersley, M. & Atkinson, P. (1983), *Ethno-graphy; Principles and Practice*, London Tavistock.

Hill, Christopher (1970), *God's Englishman,* Pelican, London.

Hill, Christopher (1993), *The English Bible and the Seventeenth Century Revolution*, Allen Lane, Penguin, London.

Hill, Christopher (1975), *The World Turned Upside Down*, The Penguin Press, London.

Hoyle, R. B. (1930), *The Teaching of Karl Barth*, Student Christian Movement, London.

Jones, P. (1993), *Studying Society,* Collins Educational, London.

Jowell, R., Lindsay, B., Prior, G. Taylor, B. (1992), 'British Social Attitudes, the 9th Report', Dartmouth Publishing Company, Aldershot.

Kepel, Gilles (1994), *The Revenge of God. The Resurgence of Islam, Christianity and Judaism in the Modern World*, Polity Press, Cambridge.

Kuhn, I. (1967), *In the Arena*, Lutterworth, London.

Lewis, I.M. (1971), *Ecstatic Religion*, Penguin, London.

Manton, J.D. (1971), *Theological German*, Inter-Varsity Press, Leicester.

Marx, K. & Engels, F. (1965), *The German Ideology,* Lawerence and Wishart, London.

McConnachie, J. (1931), *The Significance of Karl Barth*, Hodder and Stoughton, London.

Mead, G.M. (1934), *Mind, Self and Society,* Chigago Press, Chicago.

Montgomery, L.M. (1994), *Anne of Green Gables*, Bloomsbury Books, London

Murray, I.H. (1971), *The Puritan Hope*, Banner of Truth Trust, Edinburgh.

O'Dell, F.A. (1978), *Socialisation Through Children's Literature,* Cambridge University Press, Cambridge.

Robinson, J.A.T. (1963), *Honest to God*, Student Christian Movement, London.

Samarin, W. J. (1972), *Tongues of Saints and Angels,* MacMillan, London

Sankey, I. D. (1982), *Sacred Songs and Solos*, Marshall, Morgan and Scott.

Schleiermacher, F.D.E. (1958), *On Religion - Speeches to its Cultured Despisers*, E.T.J. Oman, Harper and Row, New York.

Schmalzbauer, T. (1993), 'Evangelicals in the New Class: Class versus Subcultural Predictors of Ideology', *Journal for the Scientific Study of Religion*,Vol.32, No.4., pp.340-352.

Schutz, A. (1962,64,66), *Collected Papers Vol.1-3*, Nijhoff, The Hague.

Soper, J.C. (1994), *Evangelical Christianity in the United States and Great Britain*, MacMillan, London.

Stark, R. & Iannacone, L.R., (1994), 'A Supply Side Reinterpretation of the Secularisation of Europe', *Journal for the Scientific Study of Religion*, Vol.35, No.3, pp.230-252.

Stark, R. & McCann, J.C. (1993), 'Market Forces and Catholic Commitment: Exploring the New Paradigm', *Journal for the Scientific Study of Religion* Vol.32, No.2, pp.111-124.

Stott, J. (1992), *The Contemporary Christian*, Inter-Varsity Press, Leicester.

Thomas, K. (1978), *Religion and The Decline of Magic*, Penguin, London.

Thompson, N.R. (1987), *El Lugar de Su Nombre* , La Voz en el Deserto, Caracas, Venezuela.

Vine, W.E. (1965), *An Expository Dictionary of New Testament Words*, Oliphants, London.

Weber, M. (1985), *The Protestant Ethic and the Spirit of Capitalism*, Unwin, London. (First published in 1904).

Westminster Confession of Faith (1717), Chapter III. No.3.

Whale, J.S. (1941), *Christian Doctrine*, Fontana, London.

Wilson, B.R. (1982), *Religion in Sociological Perspective*, Oxford University Press, Oxford.

Wilson, B.R. (1961), *Sects and Society*, Greenwood Press, London.

Wilson, B.R. (1990), *The Social Dimensions of Sectarianism*, Clarendon, Cambridge.

Wilson, W.G. (1954), *Church Teaching*, Association for the Promotion of Christian Knowledge, Dublin.

Wright, M. (1991), *Told in Gath*, Blackstaff Press, Belfast.

APPENDICES

Appendix 1

Queen's University of Belfast

School of Education

School Motivation Rating Scale

On the left hand side of the following page you will find a list of statements. There is a list of opposite statements on the right-hand side. Each statement is separated from its opposite by a series of five boxes. This is called a Rating Scale.

Please put a tick on each scale in the position which you think shows most accurately how you describe yourself.

The following example may help show what you should do. Say you were asked to fill in:-

| I am happy | | | | | | I am sad |

If you feel very happy, tick:-

| I am happy | √ | | | | | I am sad |

If you feel very sad, tick:-

| I am happy | | | | | √ | I am sad |

If you were neither happy nor sad, tick:-

| I am happy | | | √ | | | I am sad |

Statements

1.

My strong involvement with the work of my Church makes me feel a better person					I am not sure that my involvement with my Church makes me feel a better person

2.

My parents are always helpful and encouraging about my academic work					My parents don't appear to be particularly helpful or interested in my academic work

3.

I find it difficult to relate closely to my teachers/lecturers					I have an excellent working relationship with my teachers/ lecturers

4.

I believe that one should be solely responsible for one's own work					I enjoy helping other students with their school/university work

5.

My family are keen that I should do well and put strong emphasis on my achieving good					My parents rarely put pressure on me to do well academically results in my education

152

6.

I always prefer to work things out for myself work					I enjoy collaborating with others during group and discussion

7.

While I am interested in some subjects I find it difficult to sustain interest in all subjects across the curriculum					I find most of my academic subjects exciting and challenging and I want to do well in them

8.

I feel very strongly that my Bible study has made me more competent with academic work					I don't feel that reading the Bible could improve one's competence in academic work

9.

I feel that one should satisfaction from one's own results without comparing them with other students					I work competitively and always aim for the highest score in a better person

10.

I am not particularly motivated to do well academically					I feel I am highly motivated to do well at school/university

11.

I do not feel that my success in academic achievements is influenced by my					I am confident that I will do well because I trust that God will bless my efforts

12.

My particular beliefs set me apart from other students and their lifestyle					Although I have a strong faith, I do not feel that this sets me apart from other students

13.

School rules are sensible: I always try to follow them					I always find it difficult to follow rules and regulations

14.

I believe it is only through a belief in Christian teaching that one can be morally upright					I believe that morality and personal goodness can be achieved even without any religious belief

15.

I have never really considered a career in line with God's will					As a result of my religious background I feel I may choose a career in line with God's will

16.

My success in the exams is the result of my own hard work					I feel secure in the knowledge that God will always help me through exams

17.

I never allow myself to worry about exams or falling behind with my work					I often feel anxious that I may not do well at school or university

18.

It is important to me to do well academically so that I may pursue a successful well-paid					In my opinion worldly success is not particularly important job

19.

I don't know if my religious beliefs have made me more conscientious than my students are					I find that my religious ideals have made me a more conscientious person in all aspects of my life

20.

I want to succeed in life in order to glorify God					I want to succeed in life for myself and my family

Appendix 2

The writer Janette Oke who is mentioned in the text is widely read in North America and Northern Ireland. Her publisher is Bethany House of Minneapolis, Minnesota, USA. She is best known for three series of books: the "Love Comes Softly", the "Women of the West", and the "Canada West" series. These all feature as heroine the archetypal pioneer woman who manifests the virtues of courage, endurance, industry, frugality, thrift and hope, all sustained by personal faith in Christ. The books are the mediators of a settler ideology.

Index

Melanchthon 10
Methodism 13-14, 76
Methodist 16-26, 39-40, 42, 45, 61, 89, 110
Montgomery, L.M. 79, 146
Moody 18, 131
Motivation 33, 44-45, 49, 51-52, 56, 59, 60, 76, 82, 150
Moule 113

Nelson, John 112
Nicholson, W.P. 104
Niebuhr, R. 80, 95
Non-Lifters 102
North American Exemplars 94
Nyerere 108

Oecolampadius 10
Oke, Janette 108, 155

Pacific Conference of Churches 89
Paisley, Dr Ian 95
Parsons, Talcott 123
Pauline teaching 64, 116
Pentecostal 16, 24, 38, 76-77, 79-80, 84, 86-88, 97, 113, 118, 119
Perpetua 12
Piaget 87
Pioneer movement 66
Plantation of Ulster 61
Predestination 3, 10, 12-13, 25, 58, 76, 81, 137
Predestined 3-4, 12, 141
Presbyterian 22, 24, 36-38, 61, 77, 84, 93, 95, 101, 104, 119, 130
Prodigal Son 3
Protestant 77, 82
    Modern Protestantism 20-26
    Protestant ethic 2-10
Puritan work ethic 6
Puritanism 25, 27, 30, 127, 132

Puritans 2, 5-6, 10, 26, 28, 51, 58, 62, 64-65, 82, 94, 97, 129

Quakers 5, 93, 103, 110, 121, 133, 135

Rancher 60, 94, 97-99, 125
Ranters 5
Re-incarnated existence 7
Redemption 3, 6, 69, 90
Reformation 7, 10-11, 14, 20, 28, 57-58, 70, 126-127, 129
Religious Ethic 4, 7, 31, 37
Renaissance 14
Resurrection 20, 109, 136-137
Ridley 137
Roberts, Oral 16
Robinson, J.A.T. 20, 79, 96, 119, 146
Roman Catholic 1, 13, 15, 23-24, 36-38, 66, 82, 95, 108, 119, 128, 139, 143
Rowley, H.H. 22
Rowntree 131

Salvation 2-5, 7, 17, 21-22, 24-25, 58, 62, 65, 75, 80-81, 105, 134, 141
Salvation Army 22, 65, 105
Samarin, W.J. 88, 117, 146
Sanctification 13-14, 25, 27, 79
Sanctified 13, 64, 124
Sankey 18, 107, 146
Saved 7, 23, 37, 58, 69, 75, 117, 124, 134
Schleiermacher, F.D.E. 19, 146
Schmalzbauer, T. 17-18, 146
Schofield Bible 78
Scholarship 22, 71-72
Schutz, A. 36, 146
Schweitzer, Albert 89

160